Bellamy's Britain

Dedication to my parents

Bellamy's Britain

by
David Bellamy

TREASURE PRESS

The series produced by
Mike Weatherley

The television programmes
first broadcast on BBC1 April to June 1974

Published to accompany a series of programmes prepared in consultation with the
BBC Further Education Advisory Council.

Front cover photograph:
Steve Back/Daily Telegraph Colour Library
Back cover photograph:
Spectrum Colour Library/Blakeney Point, Norfolk

First published in Great Britain in 1974 by the
British Broadcasting Corporation

This edition published in 1984 by
Treasure Press
59 Grosvenor Street
London W1

ISBN 0 907812 56 2

Printed in Hong Kong

CONTENTS

Acknowledgment is due to the following for permission to reproduce photographs:
AEROFILMS Norfolk Broads, page 126; A–Z BOTANICAL COLLECTION strawberry tree (Maurice Nimmo), page 43; DAVID BELLAMY pipewort, page 40, limestone, page 61, Castle Eden Dene, page 64, Teesside, page 68, Coal ball, page 73, Broads, page 124; BRITISH MUSEUM (NATURAL HISTORY) ammonite, page 106; BRITISH TOURIST AUTHORITY Glen More, page 18, flint knapper, page 77; CAMBRIDGE UNIVERSITY COLLECTION Chesil beach, page 95; BRUCE COLEMAN deer (Jane Burton), page 29; BRIAN DAUBNEY coal measures, page 71, cavern, page 80, disused railway, page 81, harvest festival, page 91, wherry, page 120; THE DIRECTOR, INSTITUTE OF GEOLOGICAL SCIENCES (Crown Copyright) fossil grove, page 70; M. HIRONS gull's and puffin's nests, page 54; JOHN HOWARTH cloudberry, page 31, Burren, page 37, Turlough, page 41, boat, page 56; J. B. MOUNSEY (courtesy, W. J. Garnett) epiphytes, page 46; SAFETY IN MINES RESEARCH ESTABLISHMENT (Crown Copyright) fossil leaf, page 72.

Maps and Diagrams throughout illustrated by David Cook. In chapter 7 we wish to thank David and Christine Measures for their illustrations.

Acknowledgment is due to the following:
AUTHOR for diagram on page 105 from *Soils for the Archaeologist* by I. W. Cornwall, maps on pages 24 and 60 by permission of the BOTANICAL SOCIETY OF THE BRITISH ISLES, taken from their *Atlas of the British Flora,* and updated by the Biological Records Centre, Monks Wood Experimental Station, Abbots Ripton, Huntingdon; CAMBRIDGE UNIVERSITY PRESS for map on page 12 from *British Isles and their Vegetation* by Tansley; CONTROLLER OF HER MAJESTY'S STATIONERY OFFICE for illustration on page 75 by Alan Sorrell from *Grime's Graves, Norfolk* by the late R. Rainbird Clarke. Crown copyright reserved; ELDON POTHOLE CLUB for Speedwell Survey map on page 80; GUSTAV FISCHER VERLAG for style of climate diagrams on pages 20, 21, 22, 23 and 33 copied from *Klimatdiagrammen Welt Atlas* by Prof. Heinrich Walter, Dr. Phil., Stuttgart-Hohenheim and Prof. Helmut Lieth, Dr. Phil., Hawaii, Honolulu; PENGUIN BOOKS LTD for illustrations on page 58 from *Grasses* by C. E. Hubbard, Pelican 1954; ROYAL GEOGRAPHICAL SOCIETY for maps on page 119 from *Making of the Norfolk Broads* by Lambert Jennings *et al.* from the Society's Memoir No. 3.

Map on page 124 is from *Making of the Broads (1949)* by Jennings and Lambert.

PREFACE

The title of this book and the associated television programme does not so much imply a takeover, as a viewpoint. Presented here is an individual account of the British landscape and the factors which go to make that landscape so very varied.

One of our leading ecologists, David Bellamy delights in communicating to a general audience, topics which are often the exclusive preserve of experts. It may be that conservation of our environment is too important to be left only to the expert, but we, the laymen can only enter the debate sensibly if we have some knowledge of what makes it tick.

For all of us laymen who worked on the production of this series, one thing is certain – we will not look at the countryside in quite the same way in the future!

MIKE WEATHERLEY

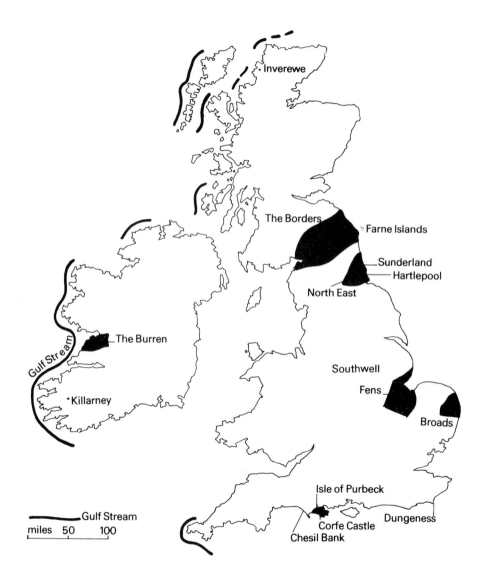

Map of *Bellamy's Britain* showing the locations mentioned in the text (perhaps it would be more accurate to call it Bellamy's British Isles but that would make the title too long).

8

INTRODUCTION

'Methinks that I will never see a signpost lovely as a tree' – with due respect to the original lyrics and to Ogden Nash, this couplet sets the theme for both this book and the ten television programmes that go with it.

Amongst the many things which 20th century technology has given us is increased mobility. This, above all else, has changed our lives most dramatically. Many of us think nothing of driving from London to Edinburgh in one day and the short touring holiday which takes in all of Britain is simply a practice run for Europe. More and more of us each year are suffering from that creeping Americanism, 27 counties in five days, "Gee wasn't the Constable country just swell!"

Wherever we fit into this cline of rapid motion, we all become more and more dependent upon road signs, most of which are inscribed with vital information: M1 AND THE NORTH – SERVICES 7 MILES – others like HEAVY PLANT CROSSING are a bit more obscure while some retain the charm of old English place names, RYTON of the ELEVEN TOWNS and LOOSE CHIPPINGS. If the nationwide plague of knocking the ends off our signposts and covering the information with spray-can hieroglyphics suddenly increased, making them all completely unintelligible, how would we get on?

The fact that the sun rises in the east and sets in the west and that mosses grow more luxuriantly on the north of Boy Scouts knees, at least takes care of the cardinal points of the compass, so we wouldn't be completely lost. Further than that things would probably become difficult.

The countryside is, however, full of natural signposts which can, if used with care, tell you a lot about your environment and hence your location. But they can tell you much more than this, for these signs are the natural expressions of the potential of the landscape in relation to the process of evolution.

During the last ice age this small group of islands offered little or no opportunity for life, it was in fact a dead, snow white world. Only the south and south western fringes were devoid of ice and a few of the higher mountain peaks stood proud of the ice cap. As the glaciers melted, the potential of each newly exposed landscape was there, open for recolonization by plants and animals migrating in from the warmer south. Each living unit was however, limited by the climate of the sub-arctic environment of the edge of the melting ice sheet. As the climate became gradually warmer, other factors came into play controlling the potential and thus the expression of each living system; factors like the amount of potassium, phosphorus and the other nutrients which were present in the parent material of the developing soil.

The linked processes of colonization and soil development, set against the background of climatic improvement, gradually developed and exploited the full potential of each area, producing the living landscapes of Britain. It is these landscapes which form the subject matter of this book.

1
SIGNPOSTS

'Wet and warm in the west – dry and cold in the east – ground frost on the hills, especially in the north and rain in Manchester,' thus says the first epistle of Bert Ford to the early risers.

Although most of us listen to the daily forecast with due reverence, the pattern of weather has little relevance to our everyday lives. From inside our double glazed semis, air conditioned cars and over heated offices, does it really matter what goes on outside? It may be nice to have fine weather for a holiday and we may dream of a white Christmas; but the only groups to which it is really important are those like farmers, fishermen and horticulturalists who have to plan their livelihood around their natural environment.

The data on which the meteorologist bases his predictions come from many thousands of weather stations dotted throughout the world, each of which measures the same basic parameters at set hours G.M.T. each day. These include the maximum and minimum temperature and the amount of precipitation over the past 24 hours. Certain stations add to this basic data by monitoring barometric pressure, amount of sunshine, wind speed and direction, humidity, evapotranspiration. The list is even longer than the names of the apparatus they use. Self ventilating psychrometers are my favourite; they are used to measure the relative humidity and are one of the nicest clockwork gadgets ever invented.

Each data set tells the expert something concerning the *status quo* of the weather; only when all the information has been drawn together in the form of a map and the composite picture has been checked with that of preceding days can a forecast be attempted. The forecast attempts to predict the continuing pattern of change. The main clue is that if the map contains an area of high pressure and an area of low pressure, then the wind is going to blow, evening out this pressure difference. The greater the difference and the closer the areas are together, the stronger will be the wind and with it will come the conditions of temperature prevailing in the high pressure area.

Space age technology has added a new dimension to forecasting by providing instant weather maps, in the form of satellite photographs, covering whole continents. They show the main areas which are covered with cloud and a timed series of them must be instant meteorological bliss.

Add to this all those country sayings like – 'if you can see the hills it's going

11

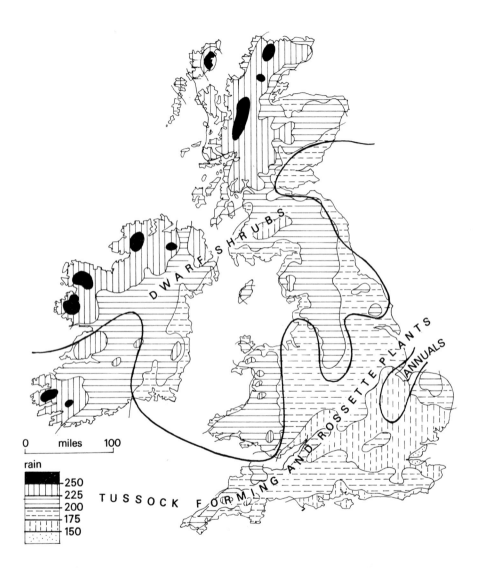

DWARF SHRUBS

ROSSETTE PLANTS

ANNUALS

TUSSOCK FORMING AND

0   miles   100

rain

250
225
200
175
150

'How does your garden grow and your rain fall?' The boundaries show the approximate extent of our three main vegetation zones and the shadings indicate the number of days on which you would require an umbrella.

to rain, if you can't then it's raining' – 'red sky at night' and 'lots of holly berries and it's going to be a hard winter' – and you have got it, long distance forecasting and all.

Joking aside, we may grumble about the weather forecast always being wrong, but a simple check will show you just how many times it is right. This is a remarkable feat, especially when you remember that Britain is a small group of islands lying on the edge of a large continental mass, lapped by the warm gulf stream and only 600 miles from the arctic circle. A position in which one might expect changeable weather.

Changeable it may be in the terms of the forecaster but there is an overall pattern of climate which may, at least in the long term, be relied upon. The fascinating thing is that if you know your plants then you can begin to read the vegetation like a climatic map.

There is only one problem and that is you need semi-natural vegetation and there is precious little of that left in lowland Britain. However, accepting this limitation it is a fact that there are natural boundaries which divide our islands into a number of phytogeographical regions and these boundaries are basically climatic.

The driest region is at once identifiable by the abundance of therophytes in natural grassland. Therophyte is just a fancy name for annuals, that is plants which come up with the rains of spring, rapidly mature, flower, fruit and die in the drought of summer. Their seeds then lie dormant in the soil until the following spring when the cycle begins again. The main zone of therophytes is characterised by an annual rainfall of less than 600 mms. In this area there are also plants which will be common companions of any Mediterranean holiday, like the Sainfoin and Sulphur Clover which can tolerate the much hotter and drier climates further south.

In contrast, the grasslands of the west contain an abundance of plants which show no adaptation to drought conditions and the woodlands of the west coast overflow with liverworts, mosses and lichens which festoon the trees to the topmost branches, some even growing on the previous year's twigs. A sure sign of the wet humid climate is the presence of our two filmy ferns, *Hymenophyllum wilsoni* and *Hymenophyllum tunbridgense*. The latter name means exactly what it says, the filmy fern from Tunbridge Wells, which unfortunately isn't anywhere near the west coast. The fact is, of course, that other factors play important roles, modifying the local climate. Just as the humid conditions found in the bottoms of the gills which cut down into the wealden clays of Kent bring the western climate and parts of its vegetation eastwards, so can sandy, rapidly draining soils in exposed places take the therophytes westwards. Nevertheless, if all the signs are taken into account, the natural vegetation of any area can tell us a lot about its climate.

Apart from the 'too wet, too dry' factor, the main environmental variable

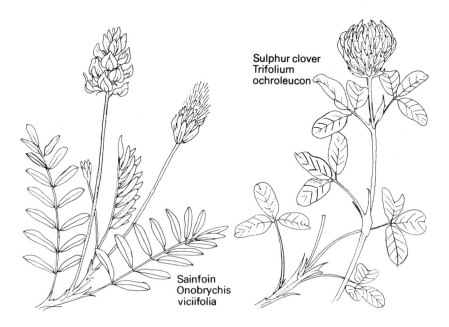

Sulphur clover
Trifolium
ochroleucon

Sainfoin
Onobrychis
viciifolia

SAINFOIN and SULPHUR CLOVER. Two visitors from the warm south.

which affects the makeup of the vegetation is the length of the growing period. There is little doubt that in the case of the therophytes the availability of water must in part determine their growing period but, in the main in Britain, this is controlled by temperature. The number of days with a mean temperature above 10°C can be taken as a very rough guide. Above this temperature the life processes of the plants can really get cracking and the plants swing into their main cycle of growth. As all gardeners will know, it's not only the average temperature which counts, because a late frost can bring havoc to those cherished early plants.

Passing north east across Britain the odds against a late frost decrease, as does the average length of the growing period. Along this climatic gradient there is a gradual change in the vegetation. Certain plants which are more typical of central and southern Europe gradually become rarer and then disappear, while others which have their main centres of distribution in the arctic and/or the alps increase in abundance; these can be loosely termed arctic alpines. However, the overall trend is that there is a gradual reduction in the overall diversity of the vegetation in passing from the cool, temperate climate of south west England to the cooler 'sub-arctic' conditions of the north east of Scotland.

Again the differences are not clear cut. Any hill, especially if it is tall enough to be called a mountain (officially its summit must top 1000 ft above sea level), will greatly effect the climate and especially the temperature. This is why many of our northern indicators are called arctic alpines, they find suitable environmental niches both in the far north beyond the Arctic Circle and on the summits of the Alps in central Europe.

So, although there are main trends and hence main boundaries, the vegetation of Britain is almost as diverse as the weather is changeable. It is therefore imperative that you must have all the facts to hand in order to reach a correct interpretation.

Another factor which adds variety to the landscape is the range of types of bedrock which outcrop across these islands. Whether it is in the state in which it was originally laid down, or whether it has been eroded, transported and re-laid down elsewhere, the bedrock is the parent material from which soil is formed. Soil is the result of the process of weathering, which is an interaction between the parent material, the climate and the flora and fauna. This interaction is termed pedogenesis (soil genesis) and the permutations and combinations of the interacting factors together produce the great variety of soil types found in Britain, adding further patterns to the landscape.

In the case of soils the boundaries can be as clear cut as the lines the geologist draws on his maps. Wherever two rock types which have contrasting properties outcrop together, the line of demarcation between two contrasting vegetation types can be very abrupt. The classic case is where limestone outcrops near granite. The former is typified by a vegetation made up of plants, known as calcicoles, which can tolerate a high level of calcium in the soil, and the latter by plants called calcifuges which appear to be less tolerant of calcium. Whether it is specifically calcium or some other related factor such as the acidity or the availability of certain minerals is not certain, but the calcicole calcifuge problem has bugged plant ecology ever since it was thought of and, whatever the final answer is, there is no getting away from the fact that the two types of vegetation do exist. It is possible to stand with one foot in one type and one in the other, which tends to rule out climate as a factor differentiating the two. Two species of bedstraw indicate the difference very well. *Galium saxatile* is a calcifuge and *Galium sterneri* a calcicole. They can be found growing within centimetres of each other, but they are always true to their rock type.

One of the more distinctive types of vegetation related to rock type is that which grows on serpentine. Serpentine is a hard rock which contains high concentrations of metals, many of which can be toxic to most forms of life.

Serpentine outcrops at the two extreme ends of Britain, the Lizard in Cornwall and Unst in the Shetlands. Both areas have somewhat poorly developed skeletal soils and the members of the vegetation must have evolved at least some degree of tolerance to the heavy metals. The vegetation of the

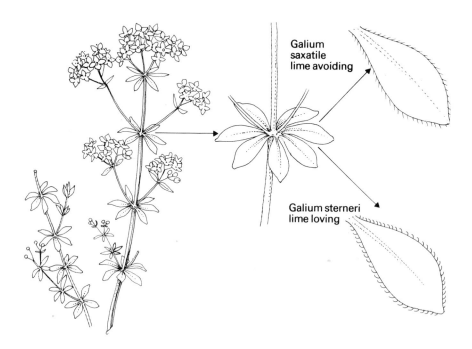

Two Bedstraws, GALIUM SAXATILE *avoids* lime, GALIUM STERNERI *loves* it.

Cornish serpentine is rich in species, more than 370 having been recorded from the outcrops and Michael Proctor, who has worked extensively in the area states the vegetation "has few or no special features". This is in marked contrast to the situation in Shetland where relatively few types of plants are found growing in a sparse, stunted vegetation. The interplay between climate and soil type is thus made very clear, one either ameliorating or enhancing the effect of the other. It is interesting to speculate what would have happened if all the world's land masses were composed of serpentine. Either the world would have a more restricted flora, or perhaps evolution would have taken a different course and produced a living system to which the same heavy metals were important nutrients rather than toxicoids.

Wherever man has exploited the resource potential of heavy metal ores, the vegetation which, given time, develops on the spoil heaps, has certain similarities to that which grows on the serpentine. Use is being made of these facts in the new art of instant cosmetic surgery for industrial landscapes. Strains of plants are being bred which are tolerant to high levels of specific heavy metals so that new spoil heaps can be vegetated more rapidly. The only remaining problem is to breed strains of sheep and cows which are tolerant of the same metals so that the dark satanic waste heaps can be turned into green and pleasant (that is non-toxic) pastures.

Anywhere you go in Britain, especially those places which have not come under the influence of man's regularizing activities, the scene tells you something about the potential of the environment to the living process and of the state of play of evolution in relation to that potential. With a little bit of knowledge, your own favourite country walk can become a voyage of discovery of the facts relating to evolution in your own environment.

It has been said that Britain has more naturalists per square metre than any other country in the world. This is probably as true in modern decimalized Britain as it was at the turn of the century when almost every county and indeed most large towns had their own thriving natural history society or field club. One task which each group set for themselves was to produce first a check list of all the plants growing within their boundaries and finally a local flora. These local floras are today collectors' pieces and the treasured possessions of most naturalists who are lucky enough to own one. In those halcyon days, to be asked to lead an excursion of your society was a sure sign that you had made it in your own particular field.

So prolific were some of the societies that their transactions or proceedings, often bound in leather, occupy large sections of the local library. The History of the Berwickshire Natural History Society which was founded in 1831 elegantly fill two metres of shelf space in the library at Durham University.

With the ever increasing ease of access to the countryside, the 1974 volume should itself be at least 100 cms thick. Unfortunately it isn't, not because there is nothing left to be discovered, for there is still an enormous amount of straight observational work to be done. The fact is that modern economics has made the Bumper Proc. Nat. Hist. Soc. a thing of the past.

This is a great pity because, just as local newspapers help to hold local communities together, so did these publications. They were the focal point of a very special community of observers who kept a record of the natural signs of our environment. Without a continuous record there is little or no chance of monitoring changes and no possibility of making forecasts as to the changes both natural and man made which are occurring within our local landscapes.

There is of course always the excuse that there is no need for us to be able to read the signs, our environment is four walls and a moderate oven. Most of us have lost meaningful contact with what is going on out there. The signposts are, however, still there and they can add a whole new dimension to a walk or drive through the countryside. A little knowledge and the ability to make simple but accurate observations, and your own environment becomes alive. You don't have to start your apprenticeship in one of our top ten nature reserves. It may be nice to stand in, say, the Rothiemurchus Forest and be able to see *Pinus sylvestris* var *scotica* (the Scots Pine) with Crossbills in the branches, a thick carpet of mosses covering the ground and the unmistakable

17

SCOTS PINE on the edge of the Glenmore Forest.

smell of Gin from the understory of Juniper, and say, with no reference to the notices, 'I am in the great Caledonian Forest of Scotland.' It can, however, be just as exciting to make your own voyage of discovery with no help from a well worn nature trail and discover the signs for yourself during a trip, say from the coast of Lancashire up onto the Pennines.

First in the lush lowlands which are so full of potential that the landscape is mainly given over to arable crops, the signs are there in the hedgerows. The occasional trees are Ash and Oak and the roadside verges are full of flowers and tall clumps of herbs and grasses. Higher up in the valleys the hedgerows get more sparse, giving way to drystone walls, the Oak and Ash being gradually replaced by Birch. The predominant form of land use is pasture and meadow which change from lush green to yellow green as the altitude increases.

The yellow green landscape itself is gradually lost, interdigitating between great fingers of brown moorland which sweeps down the ridges from the higher hills. Finally even the regular pattern of drystone walls is lost and

18

where they do still exist they mark the boundaries between estates rather than fields. Perhaps the most fundamental boundary is the last wall, or sometimes fence, which marks the end of man's dominance. This is the line between the yellow green pastures of the inbyeland and the sombre brown of the outbyeland and mountain pasture, which marks the end of man's dominant role within the landscape. On the moorlands, trees are only conspicuous by their absence, and in some favoured spot where a tree manages to raise its branches above the low heather shrubs, it is usually Rowan. While the inbyeland remains in its green-yellow yellow-green phases throughout the year, the outbyeland comes into its own only in late summer when the bright scarlet saucers of rowan berries vie with the heather flowers.

I well remember giving two German hitch-hikers a lift from Durham to Penrith. I stopped at the highest point of the road to admire the view and one of my passengers asked me 'vere are zee Pennines, zee backbone of England?' I replied, 'we are on top of them,' 'thees, thees, is only moorland.' Unfortunately it wasn't in the autumn when the beauty of the moorlands come into their own.

The climatic gradient from the east coast up to the high Pennine ridge is as gradual as the vegetational changes themselves and the best way to understand it is to look at the climate expressed in the form of simple diagrams.

In 1946 Hienrich Walters, a plant geographer, decided to check the relationships between climate and vegetation on a world scale. To accomplish his objective he set about the mammoth task of expressing the data collected at all the world's meteorological stations in the form of simple diagrams. In 1961 he produced what must be one of the largest loose leaved ring bound books ever published. It measures 45 cms–66 cms and required 2008 of those little sticky circles to re-inforce the holes which allow the data sheets to be bound together.

The lines which are shown on the general data map for the British Isles are the true boundaries, the borders that really matter, for they mark the regions of varying potential to evolution. Add to that the diversity of rock type and you have got it, the complexity of pattern which makes Britain such an exciting place in which to take a walk.

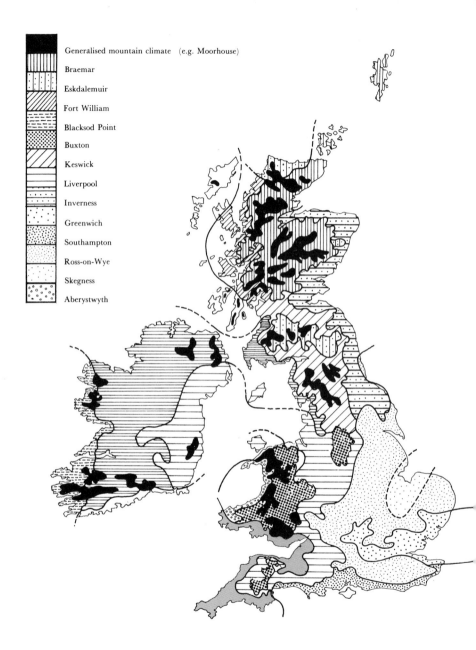

Generalised mountain climate (e.g. Moorhouse)

Braemar

Eskdalemuir

Fort William

Blacksod Point

Buxton

Keswick

Liverpool

Inverness

Greenwich

Southampton

Ross-on-Wye

Skegness

Aberystwyth

'This is your climate.' The shading shows the approximate extent of each of the major types of climate which makes a journey across Britain so unpredictable. The climate of each area is summarised in a simple diagram. Explanation see page 22.

MOORHOUSE (556m)
(13)   5.1°1870

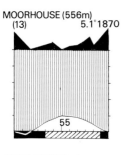

55

BUXTON (302m)
(25-35)   7.7°1233

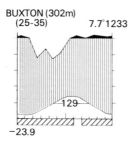

129
-23.9

SOUTHAMPTON (19m)
(30-35)   10.6°804

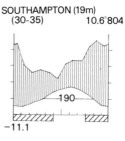

190
-11.1

BRAEMAR (308m)
(30-35)   7.6°927

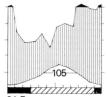

105
-21.7

KESWICK (77m)
(30-35)   9.1°1476

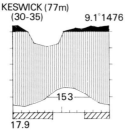

153
17.9

ROSS-ON-WYE (67m)
(30-35)   9.9°708

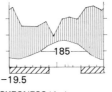

185
-19.5

ESKDALEMUIR (238m)
(30-35)   7.0°1581

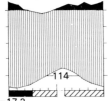

114
-17.2

LIVERPOOL (61m)
(30-35)   9.6°737

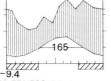

165
-9.4

SKEGNESS (4m)
(25-35)   9.3°567

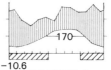

170
-10.6

FORT WILLIAM (57m)
(25)   8.3°2008

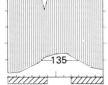

135
-13.9

INVERNESS (74m)
(25-35)   8.2°722

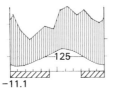

125
-11.1

ABERYSTWYTH (4m)
(25-30)   9.5°1254

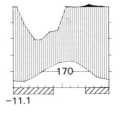

170
-11.1

BLACKSOD POINT (6m)
(15)   9.9°1321

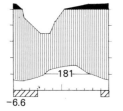

181
-6.6

GREENWICH (46m)
(30-35)   10.3°611

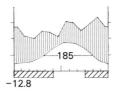

185
-12.8

21

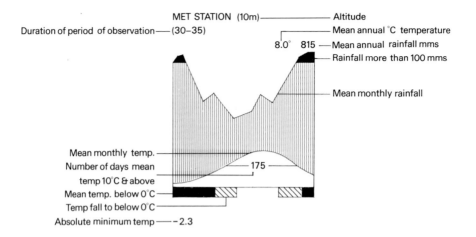

MET STATION (10m) ———————— Altitude
Duration of period of observation —— (30–35)   ———— Mean annual °C temperature
8.0° 815 — Mean annual rainfall mms
— Rainfall more than 100 mms

— Mean monthly rainfall

Mean monthly temp. ———————
Number of days mean ———— 175 ——
temp 10°C & above
Mean temp. below 0°C ——
Temp fall to below 0°C —————
Absolute minimum temp —— -2.3

These are the keys to information contained in climate diagrams.

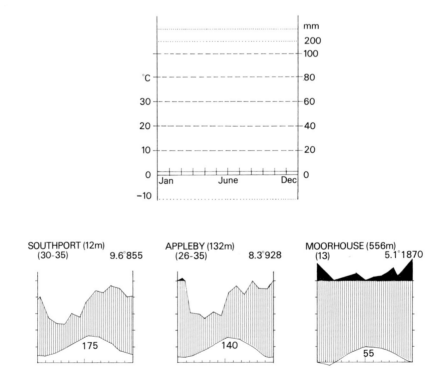

SOUTHPORT (12m)
(30-35)   9.6°855
175

APPLEBY (132m)
(26-35)   8.3°928
140

MOORHOUSE (556m)
(13)   5.1°1870
55

The three climates you would pass through on a trip from the Coast of Lancashire up onto the high Pennines. Climatic diagrams redrawn after Walters & Lieth.

2
UP THE ARCTIC

'I'm dreaming of a white Christmas;' but how about a white midsummer's day?, well most years it is possible in one small area of Britain. High up on the mountains of the Cairngorm range of central Scotland there is a tract of land which boasts Britain's only glacier, or at least the nearest thing we have to a glacier, a series of small snow patches which often last the year round. On a hot summer's day it used to be an ideal place for walkers to cool off their hot feet, now with the installation of the chair lifts it acts as a fast shrinking magnet to all would be late skiers. Snow there may be, but can the climate of this small area really be described as arctic?

It is easy to define the climate; long cold winters and short cool summers, but unless you have actually sat on the snow patch the year round, preferably with a thermometer and a notebook, such a definition doesn't really tell you much. Another definition of an arctic climate could be that frosts are recorded during every month of the year. To prove it it is again necessary to install some kind of recording meteorological station and even this doesn't help much because a close listen to the farmers' weather forecasts will let you know that many places in the deep south record frosts at night late into summer. So probably the presence of a snow cover throughout the year is as good an indication as any.

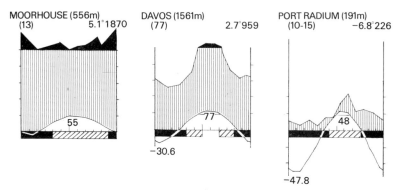

ARCTIC ALPINE CLIMATES. Climate diagrams from the true Arctic (Port Radium) and high in the Alps at Davos, and from a sub-arctic station in Britain (Moorhouse). See how much colder it is in the true arctic.

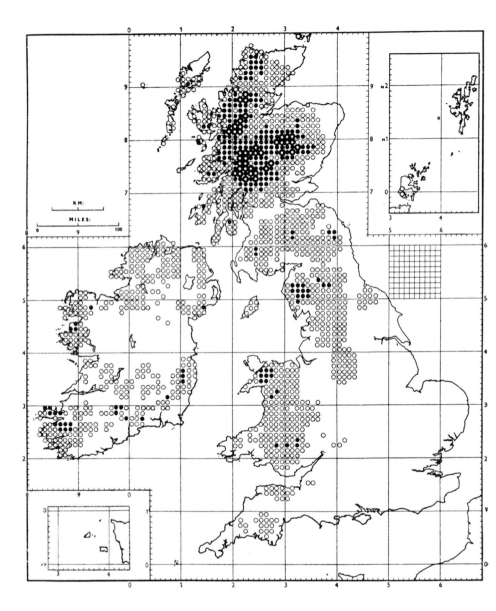

O   Squares with some land over 300 m.
●   Squares with some land over 800 m.
◉   Squares with some land over 1200 m.

This is Upland Britain. The higher up you go and the further North you go the more likely you are to find the Arctic/Alpine signposts.

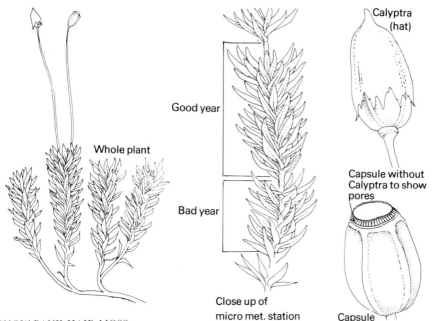

Calyptra
(hat)

Good year

Whole plant

Capsule without
Calyptra to show
pores

Bad year

Close up of
micro met. station

SNOW BANK HAIR MOSS.

Capsule

Whatever the exact definition of the climate of our 'glacier' is, one plant appears to thrive in the environment of our late and dubiously permanent snow patches, the Snow Bank Hair Moss, *Polytrichum sexangulare*. This moss grows so close to the receding ice that in bad summers it must remain completely protected from all those sweaty feet and waxed up skis.

A close look at a single shoot of this small plant can tell you a lot about the summers over the past few years. Each year the moss plant puts on a new growth segment. If it's a good summer then the segment is long, if it's a bad summer it is short and so on. It's the perfect recording met. station! The trouble is that it only tells you about the exact environment in which the particular shoot is growing. Here, close to the snow patch a few metres in either direction can make all the difference between a perfect summer and no summer at all as far as growing days for this particular plant are concerned. You don't have to go to the top of our highest mountains to find these mossy met. stations; wherever damp heathy conditions or damp acid woodlands occur the Snow Bank Hair Moss's big cousins, *Polytrichum commune* and *Polytrichum formosum* can be found, checking off the local climate as they grow. Care must be taken in reading the climatic record and many measurements have to be made in order to overcome variations caused by other local environmental conditions.

Making use of the growth characteristic of a single plant species to monitor

25

the environment is called PHYTOMETRY. There is a problem, of course, due to genetic variation in the population of the chosen plants, but it can be good fun to try. There is one other problem when using the bank hair mosses as phytometers and that is, if the conditions are right, it stops growing vegetatively and produces a flower like head of leaves which are held close together in the form of a cup which is often red in colour. At the centre of the coloured 'flower' are the reproductive organs and the cup acts as a means of intercepting and catching raindrops.

Mosses are primitive plants in that their life cycle includes a phase in which naked motile male reproductive cells, called antherozoids, are released and these must swim to the female egg cell in order to accomplish fertilization. This is one reason why mosses require a damp habitat. In the case of the hair mosses the antherozoids are released into their own private pool, where they swim about until the next raindrop falls in when, they are splashed out for considerable distances. Some of the antherozoids will fall into other splash cups in which the eggs are already mature and waiting for fertilization.

The fertilized egg does not grow into a new moss plant but into a handsome capsule borne at the top of a long red/orange stalk. The capsule is protected with a structure which looks not unlike a shaggy night cap, the capsule itself being like a miniature six sided pepper shaker. It looks like a pepper pot but contains not pepper but many hundreds of spores. As the capsule rocks in the wind the spores are released through a series of pores which ring the top. Those spores which fall on good ground (and for the Snow Bank Hair Moss, that means the damp ground around, at least, a late snow bank) can grow into a new plant. The spore must first lie dormant during the long months of arctic winter, but as soon as the snow melts it splits and a small green thread grows out, branching over the surface of the peaty soil. It is from tiny buds on the branches of this thread that eventually the new moss plants arise.

Just what factor restricts this moss to its chosen spot we don't know but this is its habitat and here it rules the cold wet roost. A habitat which is covered with snow for about 10 months each year may not seem like heaven, but when the ground is frozen solid the best place to be is under a protective blanket of snow, safe from the winds of winter. Any plants which grow in areas from which the protective snow blanket is removed by the wind must be modified to prevent water loss or else they will desiccate and die. There are basically two ways to minimize water loss, one is to reduce leaf size and surface area. The other is to accomplish the same thing by becoming deciduous, getting rid of the offending organs during the winter.

The arctic environment is thus typified by slow growing vegetation dominated by plants with reduced leaves, mainly members of two families the *Ericaceae*, the heather family and the *Empetraceae*, the crowberry family which, to the uninitiated, present problems when trying to tell them apart. These treeless landscapes are collectively called 'tundra' and one of the main factors which determine the extent of the tundra is winter drought.

In the Cairngorms the tree line is said to be somewhere between 300 and 500 metres above sea level; above this the vegetation could be called tundra like. However even at the top of our highest mountains one 'tree' forms open forest, which hardly ranks as forest at all because the 'tree' in question is *Salix herbacea* which rarely grows more than 5 cms tall. This 'mighty' tree is deciduous and, although diminutive even in terms of bonsai, the dwarf willow can reach a considerable age. Another dwarf amongst the tundra trees is *Betula nana*, the Dwarf Birch. It is of more restricted occurrence than the willow and, although it can be found at lower altitudes, its small round serrated leaves make it easily distinguishable both from the Willow and from the northern form of the Birch (*Betula pubescens* ssp. *odorata*) which is the real tree which forms the tree line. Ssp. denotes sub species and the use of the third name means that it differs only slightly from the true Birch, which has a more southern distribution. The most striking difference is that when the buds of the more northern form unfold they exude a sticky substance which has a wonderful sweet scent, hence the name *odorata*.

Wherever you are in Britain you will find birches and, common as they are, they can be of great interest because there are, in most areas, two different sorts; *Betula pubescens* with a smooth white bark, the young twigs of which are distinctly furry and *Betula verrucosa*, which typically has a rough bark that breaks up into great diamond shaped slabs near the base of an old trunk and has young twigs which are covered in small pale warts. The thing that can make them an interesting feature of any walk in the country is that they hybridise, and it can be great fun checking the characters and seeing just how pure bred your local clump is.

It is the Odouriferous Birch which ranks as the most stalwart of our real trees, marking as it does the upper limit of our natural forests. The line it marks is however not a clear cut tide line around the 350 metre contour. Winter drought may be one key factor which determines its existence, but the whole plethora of environmental factors take their toll, not the least being the activities of man which, in places, has brought the timber line down to chart datum.

However, the ultimate limitation does exist and the line must be drawn and that line marks one of the most fundamental of our environmental boundaries.

Below the line among the trees there is shelter both from the heat of the summer sun and from the frosts of winter, but especially from the effects of the wind which modifies the extremes of temperature at both ends of the scale. Just think how you long for a breeze in the heat of a summer's day, yet suffer from a similar breeze in winter.

Above the tree line there is no shelter for anything that is more than about

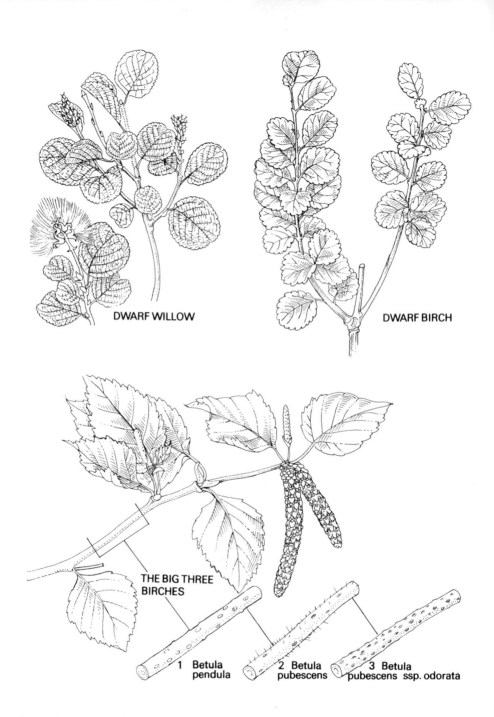

DWARF WILLOW

DWARF BIRCH

THE BIG THREE
BIRCHES

1 Betula
pendula

2 Betula
pubescens

3 Betula
pubescens ssp. odorata

Do you know your Birches?

30 cms tall and a cold wind blowing over the heather can produce an effective temperature well below zero, even though the thermometer stands just above freezing point. Never underestimate the effect of a winter wind. The golden rule of survival is keep out of the wind, and if you can't, then cover up and especially cover up your head and neck. The importance of your head and neck cannot be overstressed, the reason being that they are well supplied with blood vessels that run close to the surface. That is why you never feel cold around the neck, because this flow of blood keeps it nice and warm, and that is why, without an adequate hood, you will loose an enormous amount of heat. To disobey this rule even in arctic Britain can have grave results.

There is only one large mammal which today makes its home up above the tree line and that is the Red Deer, and whatever the critics say about the picture 'Monarch of the Glen' it does capture the magnificence of the King of our Tundra. I remember my excitement, well I suppose it was excitement, while doing my botanical thing on Beinn a Ghlo near Pitlochry when a great herd (I always say of more than 400 but it was probably nearer 200) came pouring down the mountainside. They must have taken me for a large clump of heather, because suddenly I was immersed in the great mass of beautiful animals. I will never know who was the more surprised, me or the herd!

Red Deer Stag roaring at the rut.

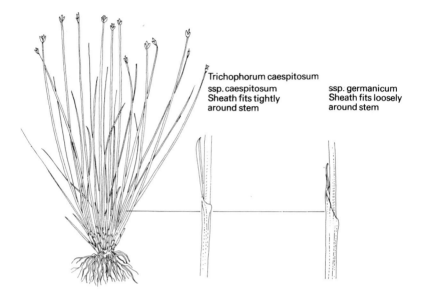

Trichophorum caespitosum

ssp. caespitosum
Sheath fits tightly
around stem

ssp. germanicum
Sheath fits loosely
around stem

DEER SEDGE. The distribution of the two subspecies is poorly known so it's worth keeping a lookout – but be very careful because they both look alike.

Large as they seemed to me at that moment, the Red Deer of Scotland are a scaled down version of the animal which abounded in the great pine forests of the past. The contemporary deer are smaller both in structure and in size of antler. Remains of the much larger antlers can be found preserved in the peat blanket which softens the rocky contours of the uplands telling us that the Great Red Deer once walked our hills. The diet of the modern Red Deer is a vegetable cocktail of Cotton Grass, Moor Grass, Bent, Heather and of course *Trichophorum caespitosum* ssp. *germanicum,* the Deer Sedge, or is it *Scirpus caespitosus*? Certain botanists have a rather masochistic pastime of revising the latin names of plants. There is a scientific method in their madness the driving goal being to give every plant its proper name, which is basically the one with which it was first christened. The problem is that in the heyday of naming plants many workers jumped on the bandwaggon and so one species may have been given a number of different latin names. The problem of the few dedicated taxonomists is to find the first one which, unless it has been changed for a good scientific reason, then stands. Very necessary but very muddling to the nontaxonomic brain. I don't suppose that *Cervus elephas*, the Red Deer, really minds what scientific name he is eating. The delicate young flowering shoots of the Deer Sedge must make a welcome change from the hard tack of winter.

30

CLOUD BERRY, the succulent orange coloured fruit makes a welcome change from Deer Sedge.

As spring turns to summer, the flowers turn to fruits and the uplands then offer many delights to the gourmet palate. The most tasty of all is the Bog Whortleberry which can in good years be abundant. The berries of this plant are black when ripe, and the leaves are blue green and entire, in marked contrast to the green serrated leaves of the Lowland Whortleberry. More difficult to find, but well worth the effort, is the aptly named Cloudberry. It looks rather like an extra large raspberry and has a sharp, refreshing, although somewhat watery taste and is crammed full of vitamins.

Unfortunately, in many places where the plant is quite abundant it often fails to flower and or set fruit. Whether this is due to a change in climate or some more obscure factor we don't know. It is, however, an interesting fact that the word Knautberry Hill is quite a common feature on certain maps of the Pennines and it is well documented that Knautberries, better known as Cloudberries, used to be sold in the local markets of Merrie England showing that they must have been more abundant in the past.

One other factor which could have affected the vigour of this plant and hence its capabilities, is the fact that much of our uplands have for a long time been burned regularly to facilitate the regrowth of young, succulent shoots of heather. Such shoots are the staple diet not only of our hill sheep, but of the

Red Grouse, *Lagopus scoticus* which is not only a highly aristocratic bird but has the distinction of being Britain's only endemic bird (i.e. it only occurs naturally in Britain).

There is a marvellous book that all explorers of Arctic Britain should read called 'The Grouse in Health and Disease'. It is a detailed account of the habits and habitat of this bird which brings life to our higher mountain slopes, wherever there is heather. Nice as it is to see a Grouse go clattering off over the heather, with its raucous cry GO BACK! GO BACK!, it must be remembered that most of our Grouse populations are far from natural, for they are managed and pampered like the best of farm animals. A good Grouse moor is a collage of irregular shaped patches of heather of varying age and is maintained in this way by careful rotational burning: 'Correct muir burn' is an art, the secret being to ensure that the fires are under control at all times. On clear almost windless days of winter and early spring, combs of smoke fringed with red orange flame can be seen creeping their way across the moors, watched by a wisp of beaters each armed with a fire broom. If the burn is right, next season's young Grouse will find a surfeit of tender young shoots on which to feed and safety in the more leggy heather which is left flanking the burn.

Using the patchwork of various aged stands, it is possible to measure the potential of the uplands, at least in relation to the productivity of the heather. The method is simple, but tedious. Many small plots each of the same size are selected at random in a series of stands of heather of known age. All the heather is cropped and weighed – this is the tedious bit – and then 'growth curves' are constructed by plotting the mean weight against the age of the stand. The slope of the curve tells you something about the potential of the site for heather and hence for the herbivores that feed on it. The diagram shows such curves for three localities in Britain and the climatic diagrams of the respective areas. It is easy to see that in the sub-arctic climate of the high Pennines the heather is much less productive than in the warmer localities in southern England. The difference may of course be only in part related to climate.

One of the main factors which must limit the productivity of our uplands, especially of the Scottish Highlands is that they are mainly composed of hard acidic rocks which only weather very slowly, producing acid soils which are poor in nutrients.

Great tracts of upland Britain are of that uniform moorland brown colour, except in late summer when for a few glorious days they turn to that almost unbelievable heather flower tint. Throughout the year the brown mass is, however, variegated with jewel-like spots and tracts of brightest green where springs bring more nutrient rich waters to the surface. These green oases are typified by a very handsome moss *Philonotis fontana,* which grows in great swelling spongy masses, and a small flowering plant which is aptly named

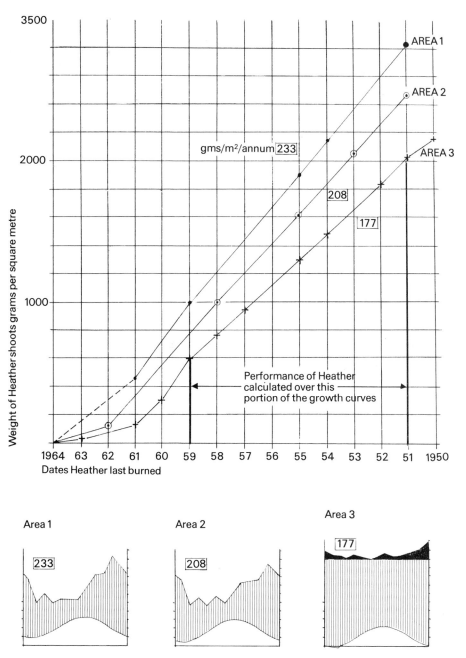

How does your heather grow?
For an explanation of the climate diagram see diagram map on page 24.

Montia fontana, although how it got its common name of Blinks, I do not know. The tiny streams and flushes which flow from these mountain springs offer good hunting grounds for some of the rarer members of the British Flora, which may be included under the general terms of arctic and arctic alpine plants. Some, like the Alpine Forgetmenot, the Spring Gentian and the Saxifrages, are very beautiful and easy to pick out. Others, like the Two Flowered Rush and the Russet Sedge, are insignificant and less easily recognised. Unfortunately, when it comes to our rarities and especially the more beautiful and easily recognised, the word 'pick out' can be all too true. Gone are the days when budding botanists collected rare plants to hoard in their own personal collections. Unless there is some very good scientific reason, they should be left there for others to enjoy. A good photograph is much better in every way than a dried, pressed specimen, but please mind where you put your feet, and your tripod and your gadget bag, while you are taking that picture. It can be just as bad if you press the plants *in situ*.

The arctic, alpine and arctic/alpine plants are thus the natural signposts of the harsh climate of upland Britain. The key difference between the true arctic and the true alpine environments stems from the fact that the latter exist on higher mountains at lower latitudes and thus the growing periods are likely to be both longer and warmer than those of the true arctic; and in the Alps the winter nights are not going to last for months. The three categories of plants take their names from the region in which they have their main distribution. The British Isles being situated at a relatively high latitude in the northern temperate zone and having only relatively low mountains, have a fair admixture of all three types.

Even without a detailed knowledge of our flora, it is easy to pick out the more diverse and more productive bits of our uplands. It is of course just as easy, probably even easier, for the grazing animals to do the same and a mouthful of Drooping Saxifrage must make a welcome change after acres of heather; and hereby hangs an interesting although somewhat complicated ecological question. Every gardener knows that it is possible to grow many alpine and arctic/alpine plants in his garden even if it is situated in a very warm part of Britain. The rules of success are simple – keep your alpinarium well watered and well weeded. It would thus seem safe to conclude that these special plants do not specifically require the arctic/alpine climate. There is, however, some evidence to indicate that they are slow growing and hence cannot compete with faster growing species.

One question is therefore raised. Do the sheep and deer in our uplands perform a similar job as the alpine gardener, keeping the lawn well mown and hence the level of competition down? What would happen if the grazing pressure were removed from our hills? Might faster growing plants then get a foothold and drive out the more delicate members of our flora? But surely such grazing would adversely affect the arctic alpine plants as well as the more lowland types. Is it climate, is it soil, is it grazing or a combination of all three? Whatever the answer it is unlikely to be a simple one.

There is one locality in Britain which is very special when it comes to the arctic/alpine problem and that is Upper Teesdale in the Northern Pennines. Professor Gordon Manley made an intensive study of the climate of the region and pronounced that the high western ridge of Teesdale was marginally sub-arctic. It is therefore of great interest that almost 300 metres lower there are extensive areas of vegetation on the limestone outcrops which harbour many arctic/alpine plants. The presence of extensive communities dominated by the False sedge, *Kobresia simpliciuscula* (which has its main distribution in the arctic), on south facing slopes which, clouds permitting, bear the full brunt of the summer sun, make it a place worthy of much detailed study. Here it would seem safe to conclude that climate cannot be the whole answer and a quick look around indicates that the concentrated grazing and trampling by sheep could well be an important factor in keeping the arctic garden open.

In order to put the various ideas to the test, a series of enclosures or exclo-sures, depending how you look at them, have been constructed around small plots of the special vegetation. Inside the fences the changes were not very dramatic, the main difference being an increase in the numbers of flowers and hence of fruits and seeds present at the end of the season. Even after a period of 10 years simple exclusion of the sheep had brought about no marked changes in the makeup of the vegetation. So in Upper Teesdale neither the climate nor the sheep appear to be sufficient on their own, to account for the unique flora of the area, and the research work still goes on.

There are, however, one or two patches high up in the Cairngorms where the presence of permanent snow is reason enough to account for the presence of the Snow Bank Hair Moss, the plant which must be regarded as the true natural signpost of arctic (or is it alpine?) Britain.

3
GO WEST

Chesterfield, which claims to be the warm heart of England, lies at latitude 53° 15′N. On the other side of the Atlantic at about the same latitude is Goose Bay in Labrador. Chesterfield boasts a cool, temperate climate and is set in a landscape which was once clothed in broad-leaved deciduous forest; Goose Bay has a sub-arctic climate and sits on the edge of the cold tundra. The reason for this marked difference is all to do with currents. The east coast of Canada is bathed by the Labrador Current which brings cold water down from the arctic. In contrast, the west coast of Britain basks in the waters of the North Atlantic Drift, which is in actual fact a north east extension of the Gulf Stream, which brings warm water from the sub-tropical coasts of Central America. This great body of warm water bathes the whole of our west coast and just licks round Cape Wrath and John O'Groats into the cold North Sea.

So, if you want warm waters and winters free of frost, go west man, young or old; but remember to take your umbrella. The problem is that the onshore winds pick up a great deal of water during their 3000 mile trip across the Atlantic. As the wet air mass begins to rise up over the British Isles it deposits much of its load. So the stamp of the west is warm, wet summers and cool, wet winters and thereby hangs the terrible reputation of Manchester.

Inverewe Gardens, which are situated far north of both Chesterfield and Manchester on the coast of Wester Ross, demonstrate better than anywhere I know, the importance of the lack of frost. It was here on a windswept headland that Osgood Mackenzie, in 1862, decided to create a garden. The method he used was simply to plant hedges which would shut off the effects of the fierce onshore winds. Loads of seaweed helped to enrich the poor moorland soils and the transformation was almost complete. What had until then been the domain of heather, gorse, deer and sheep gradually took shape as a garden of Eden in which exotic plants from many parts of the world, including the sub-tropics grow without glass or extra heating. The effect of the North Atlantic Drift is enough to keep the frost at bay.

Some of the more hardy exotics have escaped from captivity in this, and other gardens, and have become naturalized in more sheltered spots. The hedges of Fuchsia between Tongue and John O'Groats never cease to amaze me, as they form such a strong contrast to the tundra-like vegetation of the most northerly tip of our mainland.

A close-up of limestone pavement in the Burren, just to prove that there is not enough soil to bury a man, although the gryke could come in useful.

Perhaps the best place to get the real feel of the warm, wet world of the west is along the coast of County Kerry in Ireland, which is, in fact, the most westerly point of the whole of Europe. Along this coast which gets the first kiss of the warm water it is possible, without entering into the ranks of the masochists, to bathe the whole year round. Here, gardens similar to Inverewe abound and every turn of the road brings a new surprise. Most famous are some of the small offshore islands, where groves of tree ferns grow immixed with Eucalyptus and shrubs and herbs from every part of the world.

Not all the signs of the warm, wet west are man-made and our western seaboard offers some fantastic natural scenery, none more fantastic than the Burren in County Clare.

In 1651 General Ludlow, who was the commander of Cromwell's forces, described the Burren as follows 'It is a country where there is not enough water to drown a man, wood enough to hang one, nor earth enough to bury him.'

The word Burren means Great Rock and it is just that, a great slab of limestone which was laid down in some long forgotten sea and since that time has been subject to the erosive wear and tear of time and water. The hills of the Burren are bare limestone and they all appear to have been sawn off flat at

37

between the 1000 and 1100 foot contour. From a distance they look like one of those three-dimensional contoured models, but this model is for real, full scale, true in every detail and the contours are the various limestone strata, which have been bent and twisted during their period of uplift and then laid bare by erosion.

At close quarters the picture hardly changes, the first impression is that it can't be natural; the terrain looks like some gigantic rock garden, flat limestone pavements are separated by borders brim full of plants and strips of grassland trimmed by the goats to look like a well kept lawn. The shrubberies are of hazel, again close cropped by the goats into hedge-like masses and even topiaried shapes.

Closer inspection, however, shows that these formal borders are fissures between the slabs of rock, some being several metres deep yet only a few centimetres wide. These pavements are bare, devoid of all growth, but the fissures are crammed full of plants, rooted in the damp rich soils which have collected in the cracks, they reach up towards the light. Any green shoots which do reach the top and the warm dry world above the cracks are immediately grazed into submission.

This is the most extreme form of limestone pavement which is brought about by water erosion. The slabs or blocks are best called clints and they represent the harder parts of the limestone. The softer joints between these hard sections erode by solution much faster, to produce the fissures or grykes. In places the erosion process has gone so far that many of the clints exist as loose slabs of rock, which rock as you walk over the surface. Progression across the pavement consists of a series of long strides, with the occasional jump to traverse the widest of the grykes. The whole thing is accompanied by much arm waving to maintain balance on the rocking clints and a series of hollow clunk clicks, every trip.

Apart from a few very hardy lichens and mosses, nothing grows on the surface of the blocks. The main factors limiting any growth is the complete lack of soil and the drought between rains. In the grykes it is a different world, always cool and humid, the ideal place in which shade-tolerant plants can grow, and they do. With patience and a lot of clunk clicking you can find hiding in their rocky retreat all the members of a typical forest flora, from the trees, Ash and even Oak, which grow along the grykes forming gnarled twisted branches, mixed up with those of the typical understory of Hazel and Holly, which are themselves draped with Ivy and Honeysuckle. The ground flora is just as rich, Herb Robert, Wild Garlic, Wood Avens, but perhaps most typical of all, ferns, and what ferns, Harts Tongue, Maidenhair and Rusty-Back Fern fill the chinks with their own special greens. The place to see the Burren ferns at their best is on the Aran Islands which are the most westerly extension of the limestone slab protruding out into the Atlantic. Here the

38

ferns reach a special luxuriance, the Rusty Back, which is normally only 10 centimetres long, can have fronds of up to 40 centimetres or more, and here the term ecological niche has a real and tangible meaning. The Rusty Back is easy to recognise with its tough, leathery scalloped leaf, the back of which is covered with a thick mass of brown sori containing the spore cases.

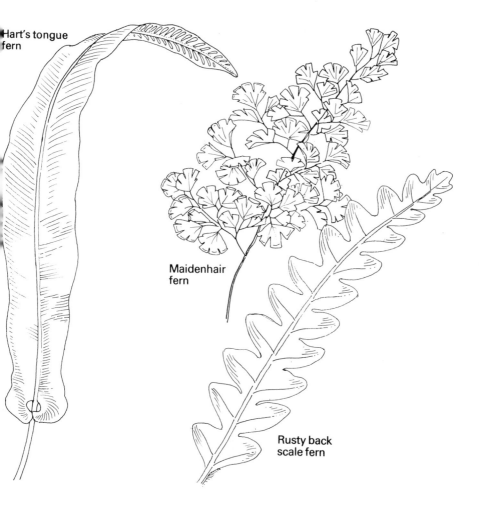

Hart's tongue fern

Maidenhair fern

Rusty back scale fern

The Burren ferns – all denizens of the grykes.

Protruding like a skeletal finger from the main massif of the Burren out into Galway Bay is Black Head. It is here that the most surprising secret of the Burren unfolds itself at the right time of year. Not far above the upper tidal limit, especially where the clints are covered with a thin skin of peat, in late spring there is a riot of colour and the illusion of a man-made rock garden of vast dimensions is complete. Here alpine and arctic plants like the Spring Gentian and Mountain Avens grow together, in a sparse grassland of Blue Sesleria mixed with plants like the Bloody Cranesbill and the Close Flowered Orchid, which range from the warm Mediterranean. Higher up on Black Head the Bear Berry, which is so typical of the arctic regions, grows in abundance and in places the Burren landscape turns golden yellow with the flowers of the Shrubby Cinquefoil. This handsome shrub, which is related to the rose and the strawberry, has its main distribution in North America. It is a very easy plant to grow in gardens and it is therefore something of a mystery why, in Britain, it is naturally confined to a few very small areas, in the Lake District, Upper Teesdale and the Burren. Its presence in large stands in the Burren again helps the illusion of a man-made garden.

Another visitor from North America is the Pipewort which, although rare in the Burren it has gained a strong foothold along our west and especially our north west coast, yet has never penetrated far across the country. The Pipewort grows in its characteristic circular patches in the shallow waters of pools and lakes, its 'segmented' roots looking like masses of black and white worms where wave action has removed the mud and silt.

PIPEWORT, a visitor from North America.

Even the lakes of the Burren are very special things, each with a mind of its own. They go under the local name of Turlough, which simply means 'dried up spot', and they come into the category of 'karst lakes'. Each of the Turloughs is a depression in the limestone which reaches down below the water table. However the water table of the great block of porous limestone is not a very permanent, nor hence reliable, feature and neither is the water in the Turloughs. These crystal clear lakes can fill and empty as if by magic, in a way which appears completely unrelated to the pattern of rainfall. Indeed one can be empty while the adjacent one is full to overflowing. The reason is that the limestone mass was laid down in a series of strata, which have not only different rates of erosion, but differ in porosity and the erratic behaviour of these lakes reflects the drainage of the rain down through the layers of the great layer rock cake. Haphazard as the behaviour of the waters may seem, they do follow an overall pattern in that during the wet winters most of the Turloughs are full and in the warm summers many of them do empty right out. The vegetation of these dried up spots often consists of a springy turf of meadow species which look very much out of place when the 'tide' is in.

Porous limestone and the wet oceanic climate appear to constitute a very special British environmental cocktail because, wherever they crop up together, the vegetation of the area has some peculiar characteristics. These peculiarities revolve around an admixture of plants from a number of different climatic regions and often includes arctic alpines growing almost at sea level.

A Leprechaun in a Turlough, just before the plug came out.

41

The problem is, exactly what is it in the cocktail that makes this possible?

The clints and grykes of the Burren may give us a clue in the fact that everything points to water erosion by solution as being the chief formative factor at work in the landscape. Under these extreme effects of high rainfall, any minerals that become available at the surface of the porous rock will be washed away down out of reach of the plant roots. As if to prove the point, in many areas, especially near the sea, slabs of limestone are sometimes covered with a vegetation which is dominated by members of the heather family, the *Ericaceae*, all of which are reckoned to be calcifuges, that is, they appear to dislike too much calcium in the vicinity of their roots.

Calcifuges growing on what otherwise looks like bare limestone appears to be just another one of those puzzles of the Burren. However, close and careful inspection reveals that the Heather and the Ericas are actually rooted in pads of humus which consists of the dead remains of mosses, especially one very handsome moss called *Breutelia chrysocoma*. Careful dissection reveals that the roots which penetrate into the moss cushion reach the rock surface and turn back, so that the delicate feeding roots are in the acid layers of humus. Whether this is brought about by the supposedly 'toxic' calcium or simply the fact that the humus holds water is still something of a matter of conjecture. The answer is probably a combination of the two. The high rainfall must, however, help to maintain lower levels of free calcium at the surface than would be present in drier climates.

One of the many signposts which unequivocally tell you that you have indeed gone west, is the presence of a surprising variety of members of the heather family. They range in stature from the tiny stunted heathers which grow on the exposed plateau of the Burren, to the lush groves of the Strawberry Tree, *Arbutus unedo*, that clothe the shores of the lakes of Killarney.

At first glance, it is difficult to see why this broad leaved tree, with its bunches of red strawberry-like fruits, is related to the heathers and the heaths. Closer inspection of the flowers however give instant confirmation of the fact that the pollen sacs are each supplied with pores, through which pollen is released, and they are adorned with appendages which look not unlike miniature horns. Both the pores and the horns are trademarks of the heather family, and one of the best ways on which to check this fact is to take a look in the large flowers of Rhododendron, which is again, surprise, surprise a member of the same family.

Beautiful as the Strawberry Tree is, my firm favourite is St. Dabeoc's Heath, with its large bell-like flowers of crimson red. These are borne on somewhat trailing stems, which creep through the other plants and pop up in the most unexpected places, often adding a splash of colour quite late in the season. *Daboecia polifolia* is quite easy to tell from the majority of the heaths, which all have the generic name *Erica*.

Fruits, flowers and leaves of the Strawberry Tree – ARBUTUS UNEDO.

The figure gives a simple key to the members of the heather family including these exotic heaths which form the hard core of this special western group of our flora, called the Lusitanian element. The name is derived from the fact that they all have their main homes in Spain and Portugal, creeping up and finding their northern limits along this warm coast. Some of them have a very restricted distribution in Britain and for this reason their localities are best kept a secret, until of course we all learn to obey the new rules of the countryside and leave the wild flowers there for everyone to enjoy. So the best way to see our Lusitanian heaths in all their glory is to go to one of the many formal gardens dotted around the country which specialise in the Heather Family.

There is no better way to understand the potential of this west coast environment than to look at the common heather itself. In sheltered niches in Killarney, heather plants can grow to a height of over a metre in as little as 10 years, which, compared to 20 centimetres in the same time in the 'arctic' wastes of the Northern Pennines (see Chapter 2), is proof enough that as far as the heather is concerned these two areas are, at least climatically, worlds apart.

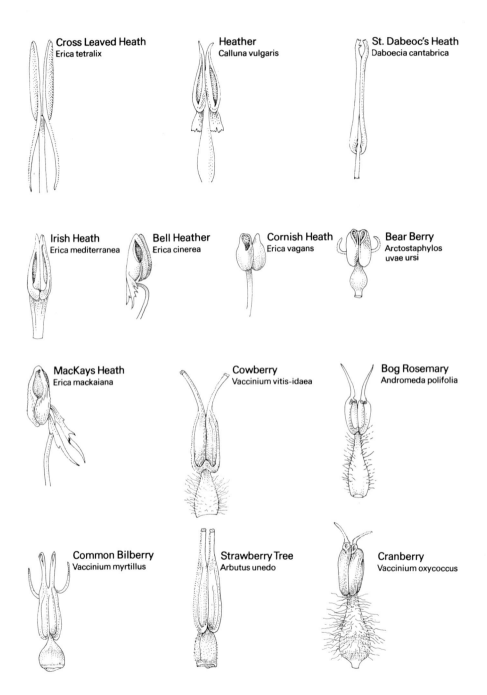

Cross Leaved Heath
Erica tetralix

Heather
Calluna vulgaris

St. Dabeoc's Heath
Daboecia cantabrica

Irish Heath
Erica mediterranea

Bell Heather
Erica cinerea

Cornish Heath
Erica vagans

Bear Berry
Arctostaphylos uvae ursi

MacKays Heath
Erica mackaiana

Cowberry
Vaccinium vitis-idaea

Bog Rosemary
Andromeda polifolia

Common Bilberry
Vaccinium myrtillus

Strawberry Tree
Arbutus unedo

Cranberry
Vaccinium oxycoccus

IDENTIKIT for the Irish Members of the HEATH family – all you need is a flower and a good magnifying glass.

44

This great admixture of plants from different regions has, of course, given rise to a great debate not only of why they can all grow there, but of how they managed to get there. The alpines are probably relics from the early period after the last glaciation (see Chapter 2) when arctic alpine vegetation covered Britain. Just as St. Patrick is said to have stopped the snakes coming to Ireland, so St. Patrick in the guise of the Irish Sea stopped many plants making it to the Emerald Isle. As the ice melted, the oceans of the world filled up once more and covered the land bridges which linked not only Ireland to England and Wales, but also Britain to Europe. It was across these land bridges that the bulk of the plants and animals made their way back into Britain. The real gap in our understanding relates therefore to the North American and the Lusitanian elements of our flora. One school of thought argues that South West Ireland was not covered with ice and that the plants were there throughout the time that the rest of Britain was under ice. Another group argue that these plants could not have tolerated the conditions so close to the great ice sheet and that they must have migrated there since. The two basic mechanisms of such infiltration would be either getting stuck onto migrating birds or perhaps being carried on drift material across the oceans. Whatever the real answer, one thing is sure and that is that these plants may like the climate of our west coast, but they have not made it very far inland, at least not on their own.

Apart from its lakes, Killarney is perhaps most famous for its oak woods, which can only be described as magnificent. 'I know a telegraph pole where the Wild Filmy Fern blows,' may not be as poetic as Shakespeare's Wild

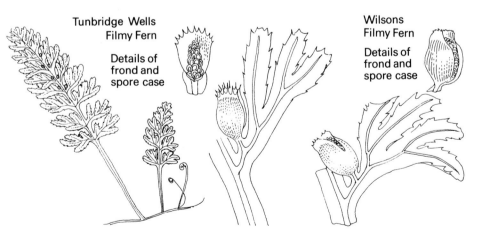

FILMY FERNS, two of the most delicate members of the British Flora.

THE COMMON POLYPODY. Our largest Epiphyte on a Killarney Oak tree.

Thyme, but the vegetation of this particular pole, which is set in the fringe of one of these oak woods must merit equal beauty. Like the trunks of the trees, it is festooned with green draperies of moss amongst which grow the most delicate of our ferns, the Tunbridge Wells and Wilson's Filmy Fern. They look more like leafy liverworts than ferns, their fronds are so thin that when held against the light they are translucent, and if they are exposed to the dry air they will loose water very rapidly, shrivel and die. In the dense woodland the humidity is always high and a phenomenal range of tiny shade-loving plants find safe sites in which to live their sheltered lives.

It is here that some of Britain's rarest mosses and liverworts grow, together with commoner ones, in such abundance that they give these woods a unique character. This is the kingdom of the epiphytes, that is, plants which grow stuck onto the outside of other plants. Not only the boles of the trees, but their trunks, branches and even twigs are festooned each with its own distinctive vegetation of mini epiphytes.

The two largest epiphytes are the Lungwort, *Pulmonaria*, which is the largest of our lichens, and the Common Polypody which is one of the only true vascular epiphytes in the British flora. Vascular plants are plants which have roots, stems and leaves connected by internal tissues which conduct waters, minerals and sugars around the complex plant body. The Lichens, Liverworts and Mosses do not have any internal conducting system. The Filmy Ferns are in actual fact vascular plants, but living as they do in the humid air of the forest their vascular system is almost redundant and thus the much more robust fern, the Polypody probably does stand alone in this category. The trouble is that in this warm, wet world anything can happen and if you take a close look in the forest canopy, all sorts of plants have taken to the 'air', growing on the thick pads of humus which collect in the crotches of the oaks. These, of course, cannot strictly be termed epiphytes.

The fabulous epiphytes of the Killarney woods are, however, under attack, and their assailant is that other member of the Heather Family, the dreaded Rhododendron. Now only too common, the Rhododendron was brought from its native home in North Africa to our gardens and estates, all on account of its showy flowers. In many places it has broken out of captivity and in Killarney it has run amok through the oak woods. The great shrub, with its many branches and tough leathery leaves, blots out all the light which should reach deep into the forest canopy and produces a thick raw litter, changing the whole environment of the forest. Gone is the damp, lush, sun dappled world of the epiphytes and gone are the epiphytes which once made these great tracts of woodland unique.

The fight is on to eradicate the dreaded shrub, but it will be a long up-hill and down-dale struggle because this is the land not only of the epiphytes but also of the *Ericaceae*.

4
THE BORDERS

Stretching across mainland Britain, as if strung between Wallsend in the East and Port Carlisle in the West, is a double line which once marked an achievement if not a boundary of the Great Roman Empire. For much of its length the remains of this wall, Hadrian's Wall, and the vallum wends its way over moorlands and crags, past small loughs, peaty streams and remote farmhouses. Milecastles still stand, sentinels keeping their watch over the dreamy sheep, the wall itself herding the visitors from Housteads to the next vantage point where history has marked the ground in stone.

It is a marvellous place to walk, whether you hunt the ghosts of long dead Centurians, the great Roman snails which they left to graze the meagre pastures of the wall or simply the long blue-grey views both north and south. It is, however, difficult not to commiserate with the many who served their time guarding this northern frontier. To be posted to the wall from the warm climate of Rome must have been harsh indeed. But then the land was much richer and there were many more woodlands in which wolf, bear, wild pig and red deer abounded. It was this rich harvest of meat, fur and hide which, in part, lured the Empire north to face the wild men and the problems of the Border.

Today the view north from the wall is changing as the southern fringe of the great Kielder Forest moves its ponderous and relentless way south across the landscape. First the regular herringbone of drains cuts across the moorland, a skeleton of change which is, in time, covered by the dark green flesh of the forest. The wall stands in its path marking the southern fringe of what is best called the border country, which separates, rather than divides, England from Scotland. The actual line which divides the two countries is certainly not a natural boundary. Nevertheless I always get a thrill on passing the sign on the A68 road on the back of which it says ENGLAND. From the vantage point of Carter Bar the Scottish landscape falls away northwards, a landscape in which perhaps the heather looks more at home, and a kilt certainly doesn't look out of place. The minor roads, especially between Wooler and Kelso wander back and forth across the border in such a haphazard fashion that it is often difficult to be sure in which country you are. Occasional glimpses of the lush valley of the River Tweed are there to remind you of the natural border that lies ahead.

On the road between Wooler and Kirk Yetholm there are two notices, one

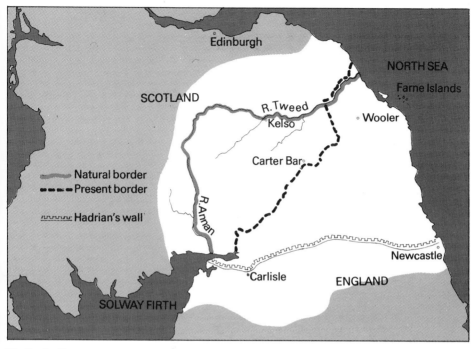

The Border Country.

at either end of a stretch of road, in which is situated the kennels of the local hunt. On approaching the halloed stretch one is greeted with –
HOLD HARD HOUNDS GENTLEMEN PLEASE – and on leaving it – FOR'ARD AND AWAY.

This is the real essence of the border country, great landscapes of farms and estates where man and nature have blended into a state of at least quasi harmony, together exploiting the potential of these rich lands.

Please, before you have me put down or send me into outer darkness, remember, much as you may dislike the whole huntin' – shootin' and fishin' scene, if the bloodsports had not been a focal centre of man's acties here, there would be far fewer natural and semi natural areas left, especially in our lowlands.

Kelso is one of the centres of what I like to think of as the evolved life of the Borders, and the Ednam House Hotel with its ordered lawns and wicker baskets full of fresh caught salmon is as much part of the landscape as is Floors Castle, the seat of the Duke of Roxburgh, which looks down on the great golden stretch of the Tweed.

Close by Kelso is all that remains of the medieval capital of Scotland, the once great town of Roxburgh. From ground level it is difficult to see anything which indicates the existence of the old town unless you have one of the local

49

D

An original document recording the sale of land in King David's Rokesburgh.

experts like Colin Martin along with you to point out the evidence. Such information as there is comes from fragments of pottery and utensils found on the site and from the curious convolutions of tree roots which have grown around, almost hiding, the ruins of the ancient city walls. More detailed evidence can be found from a few rare manuscripts which record transactions of land in the area of Roxburgh. Unfortunately, in this case, not much real evidence is available from an aerial survey. Normally the airborne archaeologist can often see much of a site in which he is interested, laid out like a full-scale map, the positions of streets, walls and buildings being picked out by differential growth of the contemporary vegetation. All he needs is an aerial photograph and he's off digging for history. While we were filming the site of Old Roxburgh we spent a long time choppering about overhead and could neither see nor film anything which gave a clue to the layout of the old town. Perhaps this is one reason why the site hasn't yet been opened up, or perhaps it's because it will be a long, long job. In fact it will require the investment of at least one whole career time. Whatever the reason, this must be one of the most waiting-to-be-discovered bits of British history.

This township reaped the potential of the region when man was really beginning to leave his permanent and formalised mark on the landscape. Unfortunately this was a border town and between 1286 and 1460 was successively sacked by the opposing groups who were struggling for the same potential. Eventually they gave up the never-ending rebuilding job and surrendered the ruins to time and the more natural processes of decay, until today nothing remains but a few stacks of heaped stones, which once was Roxburgh Castle, standing sentinal to only the peaceful river flowing beside its mound.

The River Tweed acts, not only as a main artery draining the excess water from the landscape, but as a magnet for, at least, the dreams of most fishermen. The clear water of this border river still abound with the great silver salmon. Salmon are anadromous fish. They are born in the cold head streams, where oxygenated water bubbles through the clean gravels to nurture the young fish. They then migrate down river and out to sea where they spend much of their lives maturing and enjoying the freedom of open water. Then some urge and directive brings them back to the river of their birth. Before the industrial revolution the River Tyne, which runs to the sea with the Roman Wall, also ran with salmon. Pollution has now taken its toll and the Tyne salmon are no more, or perhaps some of the more adventurous members of the Tyne population changed their course to the still clean waters of the Tweed.

I have taken to the river with a snorkel tube and mask and spent many pleasant hours pretending to be a salmon, gently finning against the current and seeking out the shelter of eddies where one can lie in mid water rest. It is possible to turn like the salmon effortlessly back into the current and drift downstream from one quiet pool to another. It is a yellow-green world of almost constant motion, the great masses of Water Milfoil heaving in the current providing refugia for the darting shoals of tiny fish which flee at the approach of such an ungainly figure. Even the pools appear full of movement with the interplay of light and surface ripples producing a stroboscopic effect on the bottom. Every movement on the surface is magnified by this moving pattern of zebra stripes, so much so that the smallest insect which touches the water is readily visible as a halo of radiating lines.

I have also spent many hours in their other environment, the open sea, where with an aqua-lung the real feeling of the salmon's free, three dimensional existence is obtained. Even here the great fish are not safe from man, for in their migration routes along the coast great nets are laid to turn the salmon from their path into a spiral prison from which there is no escape. The nets catch other things, especially where they are laid close to cliffs which are the favourite nesting sites for seabirds. In such places the nets can look like great gibbets of some unenlightened underwater gamekeeper with rows of birds held fast in the meshes.

It is along the section of coast which forms the spectacular eastern boundary of the border country that one of the rarer of the world's large mammals is found in some abundance. This is the Grey Seal which has one of its main breeding strongholds on the Farne Islands, and it was to here that St. Cuthbert retreated in search of peace from the clamour of the mainland in 672.

A seal's eye view of the Farnes is of towering cliffs of dark whinstone which are whitewashed with bird lime, in sharp contrast to the lighthouse on the Longstone rocks, which is redwashed in screaming dayglow. The lighthouse owes its existence to the Farnes, as it was built to warn shipping of their presence and the Farnes owe their existence to the great sheet of hard rock which lies hidden beneath much of North East England. Wherever the whinstone outcrops there are cliffs and a firm foundation. The architects of Bamburgh and Craster set their great castles on bastions of this rock, and far from the coast, where the whinstone forms headlands in a sea of heather, the Romans built their wall.

It is onto the lowest of the islands that the seals haul out in late November, where later they raise their families of soulful-eyed pups. Before the passing of the Grey Seals Act in 1934, this species was slaughtered, one hesitates to use the word hunted, for their skins, the white soft skin of the pups being especially prized. Because of this heavy predation the population then numbered a mere 400, a figure which has built up over the last few years to its current level of 8000. Today the scene looking down on the breeding grounds in late November, when most of the pups have already been born, is one of the greatest spectacles of the Borders. The whole of the low-lying parts of the islands are covered with the great animals interspersed with the diminutive pups, each of which must make its own way, running the gauntlet of other weighty parents, to take their first swim in the sea. The potential of Harcar and Brownsman, at least seal-wise, is almost full and the detailed work of John Coulson and Grace Hickling indicates that the population size may be approaching its natural limit. The reason is that, as the breeding population increases, more and more seals have to raise their pups further and further from the shore and thus the gauntlet to that first swim becomes longer and more fraught with danger. It is by mechanisms like this that the process of evolution works, balancing population against potential. It is also an interesting fact that the parents who do not gain the key, safe sites near the beach will probably be those which are physically or socially weaker; in this way the selective progress of evolution is maintained.

The seal breeding period is over by about January and the bulldozed wallows and flattened vegetation are left silent for regeneration. The respite is not long, for soon after the seals leave, the sea birds take possession to lay their eggs and raise their families. Guillemots, Shags, Razorbills, Terns, and Gulls, each finds the ideal, or with overcrowding, the not so ideal, nest site and at the height of the season the noise is deafening. Either St. Cuthbert was a dedicated ornithologist or the birds were not there in 676, because I cannot think of a less peaceful place.

The extended pressure of breeding real estate is having marked effects on the peaty soils, which cover, or at least used to cover, the favoured islands. One modern ornithologist, Mont Hirons, has spent a considerable amount of time on the islands making a study of the intereaction of all the factors, in an attempt to solve the mystery of the disappearing soil. He has shown that the birds have three main effects.

First, an enormous amount of bird lime, which contains a full range of natural fertilizers is deposited on the main breeding grounds every year. The soil is in places so enriched with nutrients that the dominant plant is a green seaweed, *Prasiola stipitata*. This is a plant which is found in sea bird rookeries throughout the world and is exceedingly abundant on Penguin rookeries in Antarctica. The nearest stronghold of Prasiola to the Farnes is in fact the estuary of the River Tyne, which gets the full effect of sewage from the 'rookeries', pronounced conurbations, of Tyneside. On the Farnes the seaweed, together with salt and lime, forms a solid crust to the soil providing an effective barrier to the germination of other plants.

Secondly, the birds collect masses of plant material from which they construct their pads (in most cases the use of the word nest would be an overstatement). A favourite material is the Sea Campion and the Herring Gull is one of the worst offenders in depleting this plant. The third effect is not at once so obvious as it relates to the direct trampling of the soil. The millions of landings and take-offs with little or no air traffic control, the courting displays, feeding rituals and the thousands of worried fathers pacing back and forth while the final eggs hatch, all take their toll, compacting the surface of the soil, and making successful germination of the seeds more difficult.

One bird which probably plays a major role in the disappearance of the soil, is the Puffin. Indeed it adds to the whole problem by building its nest at the end of a burrow, which it excavates in the soil. The thinner the soil, the thinner is the roof of the burrow and therefore the more likely it is to collapse. All these factors, together with the wind and weather of a group of exposed islands are resulting in the gradual loss of the soil. Mont Hirons has, from the records, traced the colonization of the islands by the Puffins.

Black Backed Gull's nest made of Sea Campion.

Puffins' Burrows with shadow of a Gull.

Puffin nesting in the spars of a wrecked sailing ship on the Wamses where there is now little soil left.

54

Everything points to the fact that the Puffins help to destroy the soil which they need for safe nesting and as the soil has disappeared from the islands so they have moved on. On the Harcars, however, where there is little or no soil left, puffins still nest in the spars of an old wooden ship which lies on the beach where she was wrecked.

The whinstone foundations of the Farnes thus afford, to some, protection against the winds and waves of the cold North Sea. The seals and sea birds reap the benefit of this protection and the potential of the productive waters of the border country.

For a long time man was their only enemy; the new protection afforded by legislation and the creation of a sanctuary by the National Trust has allowed the populations to build up in a remarkably short time. With it has come

THE FARNE ISLANDS. The numbers 1 to 6 show the series of increasing loss of soil caused at least in part by the burrowing activities of puffins (after M. Hirons). The graph shows the increasing interest of the human populace in the wild life of the Farne Islands.

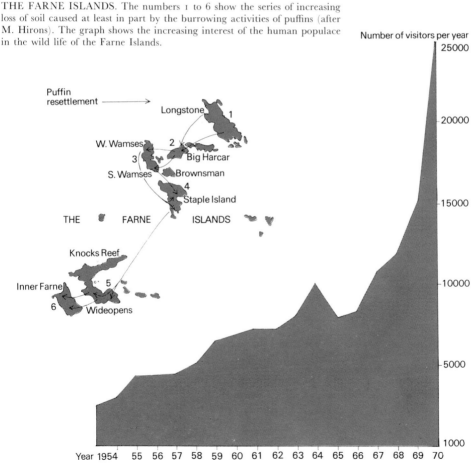

many new problems not the least of which is to control the new potential of the Farnes as a tourist spectacular. Over the past 10 years the number of people visiting the islands during the breeding seasons has increased many fold.

Sitting in the smell of guano with the clamour of the sea birds and the clicking of cameras, I can't help wondering what will happen if man's population goes on increasing. Perhaps I better put my grandson's name down for his one allowed visit to the borders!

The new pilgrims. It was never like this in St Cuthbert's day! or was it?

5
NORTH BY EAST

If the term North East makes you think of a cold windswept landscape covered with pit heaps, then I suggest that you go and take a look.

There's no getting away from the fact that it is colder up there, at least colder than the balmy South – the difference is however not all that much. (See pages 20 and 21.)

The major climatic boundary which crosses the N.E. of England cuts across the coast just North of South Shields or South of North Shields depending on which way you want to look at it. The line then runs southwards and joins the coastal strip, at least climate wise, to the region of the North Downs of Surrey and Sussex over 300 kilometres to the South. It is in this warmer coastal wedge that a number of plants which are widespread in the South find their northern limit. The list includes Old Man's Beard, Yellow Wort, Erect Brome and three

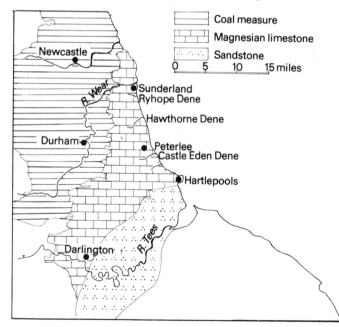

The cold but very beautiful North East. The extent of the three main bedrocks is shown, the majority of which is covered by younger rocks.

of our more beautiful orchids, the Fly, the Bee and the Burnt Tip. The latter has the most interesting history. It was first recorded on the Durham coast by Miss Wharton in 1797 and later in other sites as far North as Cullercoats. Records then became fewer and fewer until by the 1930s it was reckoned to be extinct in the cold N.E. However in the warm summer of 1969 Miss Appleyard, a local naturalist, found six spikes flowering in what must have been very close to its original locality. What had happened in the intervening 172 years? was it overlooked? had the seeds laid dormant for all that time?, or were they seed which had recently blown in and taken advantage of one of those summers, just like the good old days? We can only surmise.

THE BLUE MOOR GRASS. One of our easiest grasses to identify when in flower. The spikes are a beautiful iridescent blue. When not in flower the stiff leaves with a boat shaped tip and tramlines running down the vein make it easy to tell from other grasses.

It is difficult to imagine how an overall climatic difference of only 1°C can have such a profound effect on the vegetation, but the natural signposts point that way because, west of the line, there is a definite change in vegetation. A journey to the coast in winter is perhaps the best way to see the difference. When the deep snow is lying in Durham City, although there may be a cold north easter blowing straight down from the Arctic, the coastal strip is often deep in the slush of melting snow. The key factor appears to be that the incidence of frost along the coastal strip is less by one whole month, the reason being that the cold North Sea acts as a heat store which keeps the coast just a little warmer. More interesting than the comparative warmth of the coastal strip is the boundary itself which is, at least in part, picked out by the distribution of *Sesleria caerulea* the handsome Blue Moor Grass. The link between the distribution of the grass and the climatic boundary is in the main fortuitous as the plant follows the line of exposure of a peculiar type of rock, the Magnesian Limestone. The grass is a calcicole, that is it exhibits a strong preference for soils derived from calcareous rocks. Perhaps the stuff that is found in the N.E. is a magnesicole as well because as its name implies this special limestone is also rich in magnesium.

The Blue Sesleria has a bimodal distribution across Europe, being common on the limestone mountain massifs of Europe and across the sub-arctic lands of Scandanavia. It is, therefore, of great interest to find this arctic alpine plant growing in the lowlands of the N.E. especially around South Shields where it grows almost at sea level. I can well remember my excitement, as a southern Botanist born and bred, on finding the early flowering heads of this plant, not just one or two, but a whole hillside glinting silver blue in the sun. This was a plant that to me marked the cold northern climates.

Apart from being an arctic alpine calicole which should be distinction enough for any grass, the Blue Sesleria has one other important property, that is it grows very slowly. This slow rate of growth is a built-in characteristic and under whatever conditions you may try to grow the plant, even with all the best of fertilizers in the most favoured corner of your garden, it shows little response, doggedly growing at its own set pace. This is probably one of the main reasons why this plant does not grow on the lowland limestones further south, where the grasslands are dominated by more rapidly growing species. A sward of Sesleria thus offers little in the way of competition to other species which can grow with it, and it is probably for this reason that lowland areas dominated by this plant provide habitats for other montane and alpine plants. Plants like the Mealy Primrose with its globose head of pink flowers and white leaves, the Globe Flower which goes by a local name of Double Dumplings from its large many petalled, buttercup-like flower and the insignificant Mountain Everlasting *Antennaria dioica* the last name of which means dioecious, that is the male and female flowers being borne on separate plants.

59

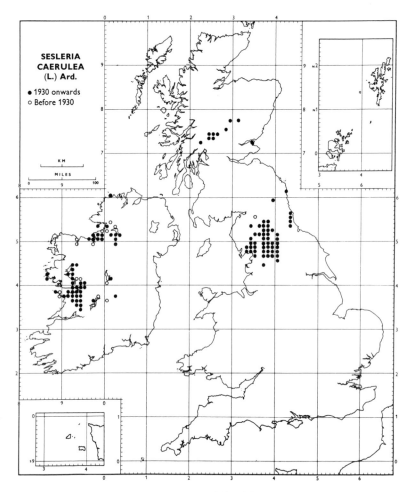

Each dot marks the presence of the BLUE MOOR GRASS in the 10 kilometre square.

The latin name of one plant which grows amongst the Sesleria, *Plantago maritima*, might make you think that you were indeed in a very different locality, come to think of it so might its English name, which is Sea Plantain. However the Sea Plantain would appear as another one of those plants which enjoys open conditions where there isn't too much crowding from its neighbours. Its distribution as its name suggests is mainly around the coast in salt marshes (see Chapter 9). It is, however also, found on some of our higher mountain massifs and in the magnesian limestone grasslands.

It is thus easy to see why the magnesian limestone is an exciting place for a Botanist to visit. Its vegetation is, to say the least, a bit mixed up, and none more so than that of the area in which the climatic boundary and the outcrop

A Broadside of Cannon Ball Limestone from Roker in the old County of Durham.

meet the coast. It is there that the southern plants meet arctic alpines and maritime plants, and as the sprawling suburbs of Wearside are not far away they exist with a fair admixture of garden escapes. The resultant vegetation can only be called unique.

This mixed up corner of Britain is also unique in two other ways. It is the home of the 'Roker Roar' and the only place in the world in which cannonball limestone is found. When filming this sequence in the spring of 1973 I, as a Cockney Geordie, almost dropped my biggest all time clanger. Standing beside one of the outcrops of this rock I said 'this rock is only found within the area which resounded to the once famous Roker Roar'. Fortunately a local naturalist and journalist, Brian Unwin, was present and he corrected me, for just a few weeks later Sunderland won the cup and the triumphant roar once again rang forth over the bed of cannonball limestone.

The best way to view the area in question is to stand on Tunstall hill to the South of Sunderland and look North towards the Tyne. From this vantage point the whole of modern, with-it, highrise Sunderland can be seen, beneath part of which the cannonball rocks lie hidden. The only places to actually see them sticking out are along the coast near Roker and in a number of places when roadworks and quarries have unearthed the strata, which look not unlike some bizarre cobbled pavement.

The exact method of genesis of these weird concretions is still a matter of conjecture amongst geologists. The concensus of opinion seems to revolve

around a process which involved a series of cycles of evaporation and re-
solution, the final product being multiple spherical concretions which range
from pin head to large cannonball dimensions and from single to multiple
agglomerations.

Perhaps the only way to tell would have been to have watched the process
from the vantage point of Tunstall Hill and, given adequate longevity and a
life support system, it would have been possible to do exactly that. 250 million
years ago, give or take a few, Tunstall Hill was in the process of formation as a
knoll in a lagoon behind a tropical reef. This was pre-continental drift and
what is now the cold East coast of Britain was then on the edge of the shallow
tropical Zechstein Sea.

The coasts of this long forgotten sea were protected by a massive barrier
reef, not built of coral like its contemporary Australian counterpart, but made
of large seaweeds which laid down chalk in their tissues, in time building up
massive layers of rock composed of what look like gigantic concrete cauli-
flowers. A similar process, though on a much smaller scale, is going on in our
rock pools today, where a very common and widespread red seaweed which is,
for obvious reasons, called *Corallina*, is busy fossilizing itself.

The shallow waters behind the barrier reef abounded with life and especially with fish which, probably like some of their modern descendants, found
shelter among the reef knolls dotted around the lagoon. Tunstall Hill began its
life as a reef knoll.

The Zechstein Sea was completely landlocked, ringed with hot, arid deserts
and it was rapidly drying up. As the process continued the salts dissolved in
the water became more amd more concentrated until they began to come out
of solution forming new deposits of rock. During the early phases of evaporation, as the sea became too salty, the plants and all those animals that could
not migrate were doomed to instant fossilization and the bottom layers of
these new rocks are stuffed full of fossils of many types.

The first salts to crystalise out of solution were naturally those which were
the least soluble and it was then that the great layer of magnesium and
calcium carbonates were laid down forming the magnesian limestone which,
at its thickest, is more than 250 metres high. These great deposits represent an
awful lot of salt from a fantastic volume of sea water. The relentless process
continued until such high concentrations were reached that even the most
soluble salts like sodium and potassium chloride came out of solution from the
water of the fast shrinking sea. Thus the rich deposits on which the chemical
industries of Teeside are founded, in more ways than one, came into existence.
Not only is the salt, potash and anhydrite of importance to modern man, so
too is the limestone rock itself, especially where it contains extra high quanti-
ties of magnesium, when it is spoken of as high grade dolomite.

I must at this point confess that I was never much good at inorganic chemistry so the next bit may well be a little hazy. What I do know is that it all revolves around a process known as double decomposition.

Every gallon of seawater contains about 10 grams of magnesium oxide. Mix sea water, slightly acidified, with roasted high grade dolomite and, provided you do it exactly right, much of the magnesium comes out of the water mixing with that from the roasted rock to form milk of magnesia. There is, at Hartlepool, a plant which does just that and the sight of the 4 million gallon tanks each containing milk of magnesia is enough to cure the most virulent bout of dyspepsia. The juxtaposition of the cold North Sea and high grade dolomitic limestone make the North East an ideal place for extracting magnesium from sea water. The potential is there and industrial man has reacted to that potential and developed one of the largest plants of its type in the world, which uses more than 50 million gallons of seawater each day.

The vast output of this vast plant is not aimed at the international indigestion trade. Magnesia has one other property which is of great importance to modern man. After cooking in a moderate kiln the resultant oxides of magnesium can be compounded into refractory bricks which can stand up to very high temperatures. These bricks are used to line the furnaces and convertors, the heart of the steel industry, on which depends the shipbuilding tradition of the North East.

It is thus easy to understand how the potential of the environment determines not only the evolution of the natural vegetation but also the socio-economic development of man himself. It was the juxtaposition of iron ore, coal and the sea which made possible the birth of the industrial revolution in the North East and it was the industrial revolution which nearly led to the destruction of the other unique feature of the magnesian limestone, namely the coastal denes.

The only natural outcrops of the magnesian limestone are the escarpment which runs diagonally across County Durham from South Shields in the North to Darlington in the South. This ridge forms the backbone of the lowlands of the County and in actual fact marks the line of the old tropical reef. The rest of the triangular sheets of rock lie hidden beneath deposits, which were laid down in more recent times, outcropping again only in the coastal cliffs. Along the coast the cliffs are, however, penetrated by a number of narrow valleys which go under the local name of denes. Castle Eden, Monk Hesledon, Crimdon, Hawthorn and Ryehope Denes cut back through the drift and over-burden into the limestone beneath. A walk through Castle Eden Dene, which is in places more than 30 metres deep and not more than 10 metres wide, is much more reminiscent of the Jugoslavian Karst country than British West Hartlepools. Karst is a phenomenon which is brought about by collapse following underground solution of limestone rock and there is some evidence that at least parts of the Denes were formed in this way. Perhaps it was the melt waters at the end of the glacial period which carried the underlying limestones with them to the sea, carving out these sinuous valleys.

The vegetation of the Denes is also somewhat surprising. The climate of the region tells us that there should be mixed woodland and there certainly is, but what a mixture, Ash, Oak, Elm, Lime, Beech, Sycamore and Hornbeam with, in some places, an understory of Yew. In the dene bottom, which remains moist and humid all the year round, two plants not usually associated with the east coast are found. The Harts Tongue Fern is extremely abundant and appears to be one of the only things that can compete with the wild garlic which is the general coverall of much of the forest floor. So overpowering is the

Part of the Mixed Woodland of Castle Eden Dene, overlooking the new town of Peterlee.

smell of garlic that it is impossible to take a walk in the dene in early summer without everyone knowing where you have been and without learning why another common name of this plant is 'Welcome Home Husband However Drunk You Be'. The second plant is much less conspicuous. It is a tiny leafy liverwort which weaves intricate deep red patches on decaying wood. Only under the microscope is the true beauty of *Nowelia curvifolia* revealed.

The vegetation of Castle Eden Dene cannot be called natural. However, turning a blind eye to all the Rhododendrons and the riot of other exotics which were planted when the dene was the garden of a Victorian castle, and to the fact that even many of the trees were introduced by man, parts of the woodland bear a striking resemblance to the pre-alpine forests which cover the foothills of the Bavarian Alps. The woods in question are composed of Sycamore and Ash with an understory of Yew and a ground flora typified by the Harts Tongue Fern. The illusion of similarity was strengthened when (in 1966) another plant *Dentaria pentaphyllos* was found growing exactly where it should in this woodland setting. The exciting thing is that it is not only an abundant plant in the Bavarian forests but is one of the species which is a special signpost for that type of woodland. It is not a native plant of Britain and has probably escaped from some local garden to find its ideal niche here in the Dene.

One other plant which is still abundant in its Bavarian setting has unfortunately disappeared from the Dene. The plant in question is Britain's largest and most striking orchid, the Lady's Slipper. That it existed in the Dene there

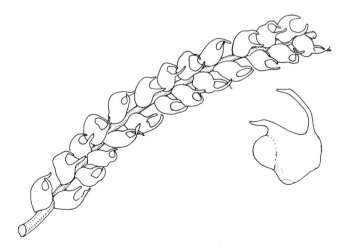

NOWELLIA CURVIFOLIA as seen under a magnifying glass. Each leaf is somewhat inflated rather like an inflated paper bag the mouth of which is drawn out into two long points.

E

DENTARIA PENTAPHYLLOS, the visitor from Bavaria that obviously feels at home in Castle Eden Dene.

is no doubt, for a number of famous herbaria (collections of dried plants), include specimens labelled from this locality, belying not only its presence but the reason for its demise.

Although the Victorians may well have destroyed the population of this rare orchid they did, however, save its habitat. The denes were not only nice places in which to take the Sunday afternoon constitutional they were, and for that matter still are, ideal places in which to get rid of rubbish and pressure was certainly brought to bear to allow pit waste to be dumped into the denes. Fortunately the schemes were never put into operation and today, even minus the Lady's Slipper, they are still very special places. So special that the new town of Peterlee, which sits on the edge of Castle Eden Dene, has become its guardian angel. The town's management committee included the dene within its plans as one of Britain's first local nature reserves.

The march of modern industry still goes on and the great furnaces have an unquenched hunger for refractory magnesia tablets to soothe their fiery bellies. The great sheet of dolomite is therefore rapidly being eaten into by mechanical shovels, which take 5 tons at a bite and work 24 hours around the clock. Here is a case of two aspects of the potential of one great resource being in conflict, for as the rock disappears, so does the diverse and interesting vegetation.

The elegant Lady's Slipper Orchid once graced Castle Eden Dene. Remember to leave all wild flowers for others to enjoy.

The new Teeside industry built on the natural resources of the Zechstein Sea.

The vegetation of the magnesian limestone is to the connurbations of the industrial N.E. what the vegetation of the North and South Downs is to London, a tract of nature's great beauty, which is of immense importance to amenity education and recreation. The problem is that the rock on which it grows is of key importance to the national economy.

There is however one interesting twist to the whole situation. Originally the bulk of the limestone was covered by other strata, especially drift from the glaciations of the past. Man in his quarrying, roadworks and other excavations has probably created more exposures of the rock than he has destroyed. A recent survey revealed that many of the best areas of the unique vegetation are around old quarry workings and spoil banks.

As the giant shovels continue to bite into the great slab of limestone it should be possible, with the right post-quarrying treatment, to continue to create new exposures of rock which can become colonised by the Blue Sesleria and the diverse flora associated with it. The important thing is to ensure that during the process nothing is lost. The genetic diversity of the plant populations which evolved to fit into this unique combination of climate and rock must not be destroyed, if they are then the process of rehabilitation will be incomplete, and the whole process of evolution, including man, will suffer.

6
UNDERGROUND

To many of us, Underground Britain is a noisy place, full of commuters, squeezing onto too few trains; and don't run away with the idea that it is a unique complaint of the Londoner! Glasgow has got an Underground, although, I must admit, they don't advertise the fact very well, which is a pity because once located, it is one of the most useful and beautiful pieces of machinery. Its almost toy-sized trains, resplendent in elegant red livery, chase their shining tails round and round the single loop of track which serves the heart of the city. If an electric railway can be described as 'neo-classic', this is it and even if it can't, the Glasgow Underground is a fabulous experience!

It is an interesting fact of life that most of our cities are like gigantic pieces of Emmenthal Cheese, most of which has been got at by the rats. Beneath the streets is a world of tunnels and tubes, of sewers and basements, some of which are vital to the living city. Others have long since ceased to serve a useful function and echo their quiet eternity away.

Many of our industrial cities are also underpinned by coal mines. It was energy from these mines which made the city possible. Their potential now gone, they form a dripping world of silence, forgotten except for the signs of subsidence which betray their presence to the lighted world above.

In Glasgow it is possible to step up and back. Up from the train which was built during the period that was, at least for some, the affluent past. Back over 300 million years into the landscape in which the energy of that affluence was laid down.

It is well worth visiting the Fossil Grove in Victoria Park, just to look at the building, which is a cross between a swimming baths and a bus shelter, with some of the elegance of a Betjeman bandstand thrown in. On opening the door, it is a shock not to be deafened by the excited screams of bathers; instead one is bathed in a reverent silence, the silence of the past. Stretching to the far extremity of this brick, cast-iron and glass shrine is a stepped platform of rock from which protrude the stumps of a gaggle of trees. The roots of these great trees make their sinuous way over the surface of the platform, and here and there a piece of trunk lies as if half submerged in the dust which covers the whole grey scene. While we were making the film, we were allowed to walk on this hallowed rock and it was exciting to think that the feet of the great reptiles of the past may have walked the same path.

The stumps of the long extinct Giant Clubmosses fossilised where they grew more than 300 million years ago. Now enshrined in the Fossil Grove, Victoria Park, Glasgow.

At first sight, the great stumps look nothing out of the ordinary, but a close look at the roots, shows that each time they branch, they branch into two equal halves. This type of branching is called 'dichotomous' and is reckoned to be a primitive characteristic; and these are, indeed, classed as primitive plants. Their modern relatives are the small Club Mosses, which today are abundant in some places on our mountains. Although our largest contemporary club moss only raises itself to the magnificent height of eight inches, their fore-fathers of the carboniferous period were gigantic trees. Each stood rooted in the soil by these great stumps which are called 'stigmarian axes', and those in the Fossil Grove are still fixed to the exact spot in which they grew and propa-gated all that long time ago. The only thing they didn't do was rot and thereby hangs the whole story of coal.

Unfortunately there are not many places where the coal forest has been preserved in such a convenient way, so that we can stand back and take a look at it. The bulk of the true story of coal is underground, where in the cramped conditions of a mine it is very difficult to stand back and look at the coal seam. In fact I found it very difficult to do anything at all. So the only way to under-

A coalfield unzipped for inspection by kind permission of the National Coal Board.

stand the real structure of a coal field and hence the life of the forest that made it, is to 'unzip' a coal seam and to do that you need a might big 'unzipper'. Fortunately for us, the National Coal Board have draglines of the right dimensions and are busy open cast mining in many places, thus giving us a chance to take a long, not so close, look at the whole thing.

From a distance, it is possible to see the layers of coal sandwiched between shales and other rock strata; in fact the whole face looks like a gigantic liquorice allsort! The black layers are the coal, which was laid down while the forest thrived in the waterlogged soil of a vast tropical swamp. Then, due to coastal subsidence or some other natural phenomenon, the forest was flooded with water, in which new sediments were deposited. Again the conditions changed and the forest grew again, once more producing another layer of organic matter. So it went on; the layers getting compressed, the sediments forming shale and mudstone, the organic matter compressed into coal.

Coal is the fossilized excess of thousands of years of photosynthesis of a whole group of plants all of which are now extinct, lost in the continuing struggle for existence. Whether it was the fact that these coal-forming plants

Careful what you throw on the fire. An impression of a fern perfectly preserved in every detail in coal.

were too set in their ways and could not adapt to the changing environment, or that the new and better plant designs in the evolutionary production line eventually ousted the coal-forming plants from their position of supremacy, we do not know. We do know that their modern counterparts, the contemporary Club Mosses and Horsetails, are very small compared to their carboniferous forefathers.

Our knowledge of the coal flora is extremely detailed, thanks to the abundant fossils which are found in the great rock cake and to generations of patient and dedicated palaeontologists who read their secrets. The coal itself yields few large fossils, the partial decay and subsequent compression having been enough to disrupt most large structures. So the main source of information found in the actual coal come from impressions of leaves and stems which were squashed flat in the process. Some of these are, however, so perfect in every detail that they look not unlike a pressed plant from a modern herbarium. If you still use raw coal (you know, the real stuff that has smoke in it), then it is well worth looking at the larger lumps before throwing them on the fire!

The detailed information regarding the structure of the plants is obtained from specialised structures called 'Coal Balls'. These are found only in certain coal seams in certain coalfields and each one is a memory bank, rather like a fossilized video-tape of what the inside of the plant really looked like. Coal balls were formed in places where water charged with chalk trickled down into the deposits forming on the floor of the swamp forest. Where the lime-rich water got ponded up in the large cracks, it fossilized any plant material present, preserving it down to the last detail.

The only problem about the fossil 'video-cassettes' is that play-back is far from instant! I must confess that I always found history tough going, but of all historical records, these are among the toughest to open. First the coal ball must be cut in half with a diamond-edged cutting wheel. This is like a small circular saw, the edge of which is not set with teeth, but is studded with minute diamonds. Once halved, the fresh-cut face is dipped into hydrochloric acid which etches away the chalky material, leaving the organic matter standing proud of the surface of the block. After washing the acid away, a quick coat of collodion (which is not unlike thick nail-varnish) is applied and allowed to dry. The collodion is then peeled off the surface, bringing the organic matter with it. The film can then be examined under a microscope and the detail is fantastic! It is from the study of such peels that we know that the modern Horsetails and the Club Mosses are related to these extinct giants.

How to open a Carboniferous Data Bank.

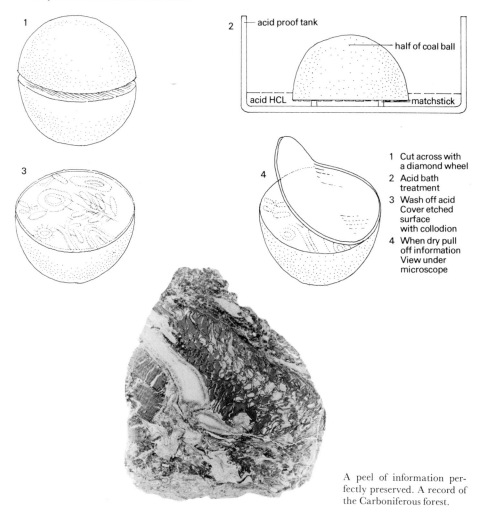

1 Cut across with a diamond wheel
2 Acid bath treatment
3 Wash off acid Cover etched surface with collodion
4 When dry pull off information View under microscope

A peel of information perfectly preserved. A record of the Carboniferous forest.

It is from fossils like this, that the whole story of coal has been pieced together and it really is a job of piecing together! The trouble is that you rarely, if ever, find all the different parts of the same plant joined up. In one coal ball you may find a leaf; so you describe it and give it a Latin name. Later you find a stem and name that; then a fruit and so on. Finally you find the various bits all joined up in various permutations and combinations until you have articulated the whole thing. Then, of course, you have finally to christen it, and the book of rules says that you take the first name of the first named piece and the last name of the last named piece and join them together, publishing the 'banns' of union.

The fossilized excess of the potential of the past landscape, together with all the information it contains, has been torn from the earth to feed the fires of the new industrial landscapes. To tap this energy, man has reached further and further into the earth, leaving behind the silent, dripping galleries which come to be known as the 'old man's workings'.

Long before the industrial revolution, stone age man had been tunnelling his way into the ground in search of raw material for his industry and that raw material was Flint. In Thetford Chase, in Suffolk, there is a regular rabbit warren of flint workings, which are known as Grimes Graves. Each flint working consists of a central shaft, about the shape of one of those concrete cooling towers, which reaches down into the bedrock of chalk. At various levels in the chalk, flint nodules are found in narrow bands, the highest class, black flint, being near the floor-level of the shaft. The early miners then drifted a maze of tiny passages out from the bottom of the shaft, collecting the flints as they went. All this massive excavation was carried out using muscle power, the most sophisticated digging tool being a deer's antler. Crawling about in the minute galleries is the best way of learning what a blackboard-duster must feel like; a white layer of chalk dust just grows on you – all over! One also begins to realise that these early miners must have been much smaller people than their modern day, 'M registration' counterparts!

Flint is almost pure Silica, which, in all probability originated as the skeletons of sponges that lived in the sea, with the microscopic animals called FORAMINIFERA, the skeletons of which form the bulk of the chalk. The theory is that the silica spicules went back into solution, only to be reprecipitated as conditions in the developing chalk strata changed. The flint comes in the most bizarre shaped nodules and, if you are lucky, it is possible to find, inside them, fossils of sea urchins and other marine creatures. My favourites are, for obvious reasons, Bellemnites which, although they look like the tops of ball-point pens, are the shells of a long defunct type of Squid which thrived in the chalk seas.

The massive scale of the prehistoric flint workings shows just how important the resource was to man. Here was a stone that could be shaped into cutting edges by the simple process of flaking. Flint arrow-heads, spear-heads, and

Prehistoric miners at work creating one of Grimes Graves.

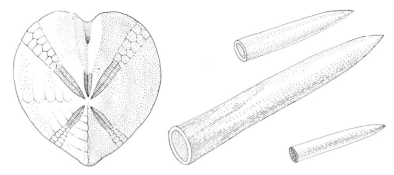

Fossils from the chalk. One Sea Urchin and three Bellemnites.

axes made man master in the original forest of East Anglia. Here in Thetford Chase, the best flaking flint was found in enough abundance for it to be exported to willing buyers who lived a long way from Thetford. So the first import/export industry based on mining was set up.

We may have progressed a long way since then, but our economy still centres on an import/export system; the keystone in the chain is the region or country which has the required resource, be it iron-ore, oil or flint.

In other ways we have slipped a long way back, because all evidence goes to show that, once one mine was worked out, the neolithic flint miners moved on to dig another shaft. Instead of leaving a dangerous hole and a pit heap, the rubble out of the new shaft went back to fill the old one! The proof is simple; modern excavation of the pits has shown that the infill is upside down, the youngest strata being at the bottom of the shaft and the oldest at the top. We are, only now, relearning to keep our countryside beautiful and the modern massive landscape surgery costs an awful lot of money.

One interesting fact is that flint working is still going strong in the area and, with that long history, it well deserves an Award for British Industry. It is also the only industry in which it is the 'done thing' to be caught knapping. Knapping, that is the splitting of the flint nodules, is the core of the industry and, like most skilled crafts, it will never die because of lack of orders but because of lack of craftsmen. Flints are used mainly for decorative facing of walls and buildings; but there is still a steady demand for flint for tinderboxes and even for flint fish hooks, which must, I suppose, be the ideal thing for catching fossil fish.

It is a fact that, almost wherever we go in our countryside, new vistas of underground Britain are being created down below our very feet. Many of these are by man but, wherever the bedrock is limestone, completely natural processes of solution and erosion are mining the rock away. It is a slow process but the end results can be more spectacular than most of our more rapid excavations.

76

A flint knapper at work in Brandon Suffolk.

The great cave systems of Britain are well known, drawing millions of tourists to 'ooh' and 'aah' their way through fairy-lit echoes. The men who guide you around the caves are among some of the greatest showmen in the world; that story about "Mickey Mouse – he's just gone behind that stalactite" always sounds, not only plausible, but just as exciting as the first time he told it. I must be a sucker for guided tours down holes and always, to me, the highlight of the whole thing is when the guide quietens the party and then switches off the lamp; that is *total* darkness – the real story of underground Britain; for upstairs in the open it never gets that dark, even on the blackest night.

This total darkness that you feel because, certainly, you cannot see, was the environment of the caves until man brought light-energy from the world above. Wherever lights have been installed and there is a supply of water, the rocks soon become green with a growth of microscopic algae. Around the more permanent lights, mosses and even ferns thrive, adding splashes of colour and life to what is otherwise a dead world. This is perhaps, the most extreme proof of the rule that, wherever there is water and light, the potential of the environment will be used by the life process. Although the cave gardens are key talking points for the cave guide, the green covering of chlorophyll is a problem in the show caves because we dwellers of the brighter world come down here to see rock, not greensward; we have enough of that in our own environment! The problem is so bad in some cases that the stalactites and stalagmites are regularly doctored with algicide to keep them clean.

Stalactites and -mites are rather like potato crisps – it is difficult to find anyone who does not like them. It is also difficult to find anyone who knows which is which! Like the tail of the T in tites, they hang down; while the points of the M in mites, they stand up. (Or is it the other way round?) Whichever it is, they are nice things and, although the glass and metal cages which surround the more choice specimens are annoying, without them the work of thousands of years of dripping water would be ruined, to be hoarded in someone's private collection.

The majority of people who visit the caves stoke up with a Bakewell Tart or two, or a Cheddar Butty and then tread the well-worn floodlit paths to see only a minute part of natural underground Britain. They rarely, if ever, see the colourless fish and shrimps which lead a blind existence in the underground rivers, feeding on plants, animals and debris that are washed in with the rain. They also rarely see the modern cavemen who work away, making their meticulous maps and their exciting discoveries. They are often there working not far, as the rock-borer bores, from the light of the show caves, but usually many hundreds of hard, crawling, scrabbling, squeezing, cold, wet yards along tiring, water-worn passages, into which they carry the potential of light for the first time.

One such man is Ken Pearce, a dedicated speleologist and one of the even smaller clan of the cave divers. It takes a special sort of person to enjoy squeezing through holes that are too small; to do it underwater, in pitch darkness, to the average mind verges on lunacy. The real problem is that, however carefully you go, the silt that covers the bottom of the tunnels gets all stirred up and visibility, even with a torch is absolutely nil. I well remember asking Ken, after a cave-diving trip in Cuba, what it was like. His reply was "Not much good, the water was warm and no sediment, so I could even see which way up I was!" Of course, it takes somewhat more than a determined, masochistic spirit! Careful training and a sound knowledge of the cave environment are essential. What, to the uninitiated, looks like a layer of solid rock on the roof of a tunnel, may be soft silt which was laid down on the roof when the tunnel was full of water. In the same way, sediment on the floor could hide a pitfall or a new side passage.

If it wasn't for people like Ken, many of our underground secrets would remain secrets, locked away behind sections of the caves that are always full to the roof with water. The excitement of diving into a new section of flooded cave is that it may be a syphon and, beyond the water lock, there may be a new world of stalactites and -mites, waiting to be lit for the first time.

It was Ken Pearce who introduced me to his upside down world in the caves near his home in Derbyshire. The whole thing started in an upside down way, because we had to get our lights and all the camera gear into the Speedwell Cavern near Castleton, in order to be able to make the programme. The entrance is through an old mine, the main adit of which is partly flooded, and the mode of transport is a large, flat-bottomed boat, propelled by foot power against the low roof. The miners dug this long passage in search of lead and they found more than they bargained for. I can imagine their excitement, once the dust had cleared after one of the many rock-blasting charges, when they saw for the first time, a large, gaping, black void. They had indeed cut into a gigantic cave chamber, about half way between the roof and the floor, the latter being occupied by a lake. The ironical fact was that the minerals they were seeking had once been present in what is now the inner space of the cave, but they had been eroded away by the water which formed the great hole. The miners had not found their lead, but instead one of the great chambers of our underground.

Undaunted, they drove their shaft further on, using the lake as a dumping ground for the rubble. They hit more caves and more water, which flooded their adits. However, they turned even this into advantage and used boats to remove the useless rock. Forty thousand tons of it were dumped into the lake in the great cave and it just disappeared, swallowed up by the water; and so the lake became known as the Bottomless Pit. Whether all that spoil is still down there or has been washed away by the action of underground water is

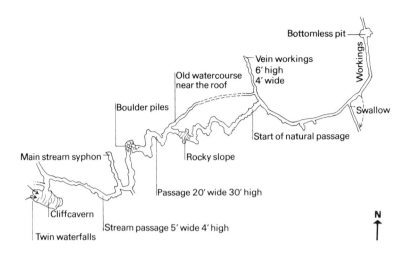

Bottomless pit

Vein workings
6' high
4' wide

Workings

Old watercourse
near the roof

Swallow

Boulder piles

Start of natural passage

Main stream syphon

Rocky slope

Passage 20' wide 30' high

Cliffcavern

Stream passage 5' wide 4' high

Twin waterfalls

N

not known. Either way, it shows the power of underground water as an erosive force.

So the story of this particular underground exploration went on, and is indeed still going on. The mines link up with other caves and, on dry weekends, the rock is alive with the grunts and groans of the speleologists at their chosen pastime in their own dark world. The exciting thing that keeps them going is that next weekend, they may find a bigger and better cave in the labyrinth of underground Britain.

Exit Ken Pearce doing it the hard way underwater in Speedwell Cavern.

7
DAVID'S MEADOW

This chapter, and come to that the programme that goes with it, differs from all the others because it is about one very small part of Britain. It is not even the most exotic part, nor is it the most beautiful, nor the most way out, nor indeed the most anything. It's just an ordinary bit of our countryside, so ordinary that I would like to bet that wherever you live there will be a tract of similar land nearby.

What's more it's not my meadow, I'm not the David in the title and just to round this whole negative thing off, its not even a meadow. David's Meadow is, in actual fact, a strip of disused railway track just outside Southwell in Nottinghamshire. It's a nice place for a dog to walk its more energetic type of master, an illicit way to get your car to the local race track, and an ideal place to dump those larger species of household ephemereta that the dust bin man never seems to want.

Struck from the lists of timetables of British Rail, David's Meadow now works to a much more stringent timetable, that of the environment.

F

The railway used to curve its way through the water meadows of the River Trent on a high embankment topped with clinker. In the crook of the curve is the local rubbish dump which adds its own foetid vapours to the mists which creep up from the river. Yet even this great mass of smouldering decay adds variety to the landscape, attracting flights of gulls which vie with the crows for the carrion that falls from the tables of Southwell. But Southwell itself has fallen from the tables, the time tables of British Rail. Axed by Beeching, the high bank stands silent, left to nature, in a landscape in which there is little or nothing left which can be called natural. The local scene is of ordered fields, farmed green to their productive edges, contained by tarmacadam roads with neat well kept verges.

It was along such a road that late on a summer's day David Measures rode his bike across the bridge which now spans the silent bank. He saw a small butterfly fly over the parapet and down towards the track. Having had an interest in butterflies for much of his life, he dropped his bike and gave chase. He found the butterfly, a Wall, sunning itself exactly where a butterfly of that name should on the sun-warmed brickwork of the bridge, but he found much more than that. A living workshop which was to occupy his time and many talents for years to come.

This chapter is about this piece of waste land, which I have called David's Meadow, and whatever I write about it, it will be inadequate as most descriptions of natural phenomena are. There is only one way to really find out what it is all about and that is to experience it on a guided tour with David Measures himself, and second best is to look at the detailed record of the life of the meadow which David has kept for the past five years. Come rain or shine David has stalked the meadow in much the same way that a cat stalks a mouse. He stays quite still, close to the ground while he makes rapid sketches recording exactly what his insects are up to, what, when and how they eat, then he darts on, either following the same insect in its perambulations, or distracted by another whose dossier is still incomplete. Each page of his sketch pad is an intricate account, not only of the insect's life but of the artist's rapport with that insect. It is just like opening up one of the Disney Wild Life Adventures, it's all happening on the pages, they glow with life. The really fascinating thing is that beautiful as the pictures are, it is the intricate notes, woven onto the page, which makes it all come truly alive.

David has let me include, a few of his five hundred pages of living record in this book. They are not special ones, just two days of observation on a piece of land for which man has no longer any use. They tell their own story and need no expansion by me, so what I am going to do is tell you what I have learned from David and his Meadow.

One reason I became a Botanist and not a Zoologist is that plants stand still to be studied while animals rush about all over the place. You see basically I

(text continues page 86)

F.T. 21st June. midday, warm wind, cloud & some sun.   Thursday   55°F during cloud ~ rising full periods of sunshine.   S.E. up the track.

After moon waning, Sat night deterioration in weather & last 2 days rain
3. in garden weathope 11.15 a very tattered g.v.w. feeding on sweet rocket.)
mother, Fisherton rd. verge, also tattered.
~ entrance, no longer perfect while flying about the bushes of dog roses.
the L. skipper ♂ still parading entry & sent off another, twirling up into the
hawthorns than returns to low leaf to perch, gleaming gold.
Larger & dark brown's butterfly flew past quickly & up into hawthorns? meadow brown.

up in a moment & chasing off a
hoverfly; settling to feed now~
then on bramble, also on the
wild briar
another cock came thro' & was sent off
beyond the gate.

the sooty brown butterfly again
flying about the hawthorns
as tho' about to settle
& chased off by this ♂
L. skipper.

Once on the track verge
L. skippers are plentiful &
feeding hard from
bramble & hawkbit.
One sitting quiet ejected speck of waste
from anus. orange coloured.
2 sm. coppers tumbling &
twirling & settling close to
each other.
meadow brown landed on cinders
& sat quietly closed.
other insects numerous, & flys
about my face including the bright
green & crimson fly.

g.v.w. ♂ feeding
from hawkbit &
briars

♂

One of the 2 coppers very small &
jewel like, the other more yellow &
slight tear at wing bases, she settled
on piece of silver paper.

m. brown hugging the cinders.
you'll look & be sure it's not there...
closed & crouching & tilted as sheath
it's good e.g. of vanishing.
Another, flying down the track flew
right over it & still it didn't stir;
& blows slightly in breeze.

& fly,
gup,
black body
dics on bramble.

& sun strong & hot — it changes its position
at it L's foot.
I think a hen.

then changes
again.

Some details from David Measures' sketch book. The results of patient observations over two days.

ent:-
ld Fiskerton
track
.6. 73
pm

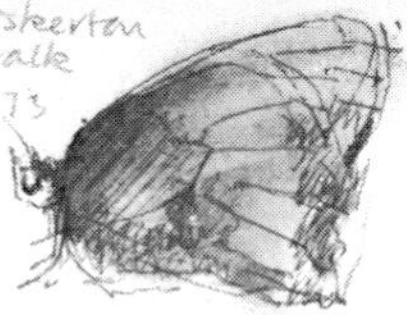

the ♀ m.b. during long
interval of cloud crouched
in crubers, sometimes disturbed
up flying into trees by track
it always came back to perch closed up, on ground.
sometimes moving, to clean one of the antenae.
With the flush of L.skippers in the brambles & appearance of meadowbrowns
the miniature willowherb & pink bindweeds have come into flower.
.15

a ♀ skipper
fanning out
like a moth,
not once doing
its bi-plane
position
feeding from bramble flowers
1 after the other.

- a slightly
, tattered
s. heath
½ way to lre.
dyke.

A dull cock m.b.
chased & feeding
with the L.skippers
went to feed
on same bramble
flower as a ♀ sitting
quiet; she shimmered
& he persisted as tho'
wishing to mate
with her! A ♂ L.skipper
came & tried to seng himself
but he was unmoved &
after feeding again went back to try again!

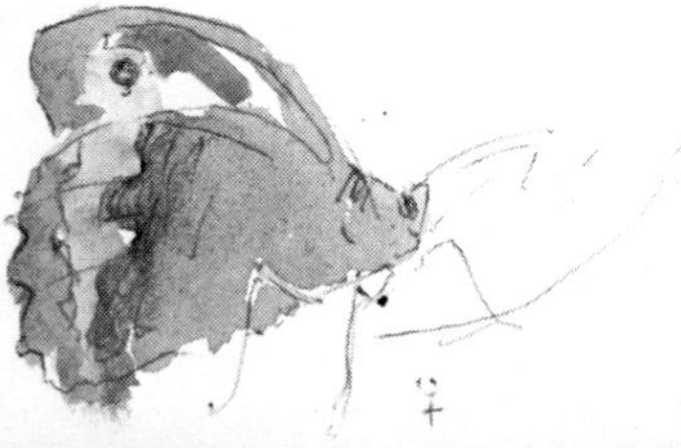

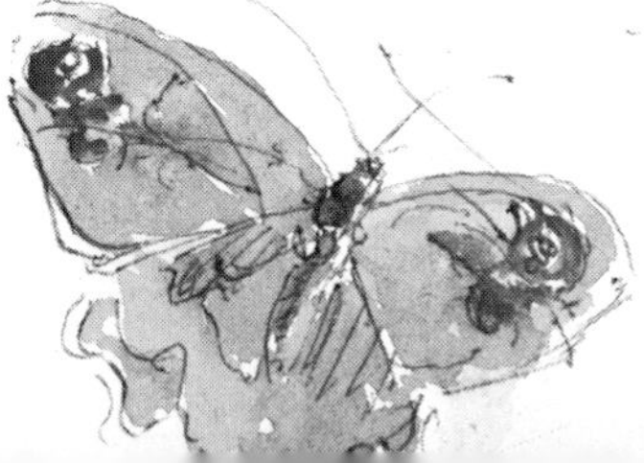

am a lazy biologist, if the plant was fixed to a certain spot one year then there's every likelihood that it will be there waiting for me next year. Not so I thought, with the animals, especially the insects. The only insects I can always find, whether I want to or not, are mosquitos, midges and clegs, but all the others take a lot of finding. Just how wrong can you be? Many insects which have made their home on the branch line frequent particular flowers for their food and different plants on which to lay their eggs.

Plants like the Toadflax which has flowers like a miniature Snapdragon and stores its nectar in the bottom of a yellow spur is pollinated mainly by large fat bees. Out of all the insects, only these heavyweights are heavy enough to open the flower and bulldoze their way down to the food although Brimstone butterflies with their long tongues can reach in and steal it. At the other end of the scale the tiny open flowers which make up the great creamy saucers of the Elder give off a sweet and sickly scent and are pollinated by tiny flies. So if the plants stay put, so do the insects. All you need is a measure of patience. Even the time of day gets into the act. The evening primrose opens its handsome flowers, as its name suggests, in the evening, and there, ready and waiting for breakfast, are the night flying moths. Perhaps most surprising of all is the fact that it's not only the different sorts of insects which have their own special patch. Many of the individuals have their own territories, and just like the territorial birds they beat the bounds, chasing away would-be intruders.

Part of David's notes are not about the big flamboyant insects, the large butterflies and moths. They concern the lives of the smaller and more insignificant ones, about the lives of which even the top brass of the insectologists know very little. One of the reasons for this lack of knowledge is that there are an awful lot of insects and relatively very few observers.

The really exciting thing is that wherever we live there is a David's or Fred's or Gillian's or Ann's Meadow waiting for someone to unravel its mysteries. David Measures has proved that you don't have to be a trained-ologist to be able to do just that. If you are using the excuse that I did "I can't draw," well forget it!

I have always been very envious of people who have artistic talent, because I don't. So I invested in a camera, but it was still no good. My photographs of flowers and insects were as dead as the photographic paper on which they were printed. So I have taken a leaf out of David's record book and have started to write notes all over my photographs, and they are beginning to come alive. Perhaps it's just the fact that I am spending more time on them and I get more involved, I don't know. Even more exciting, I have once again invested in a sketch pad and I try to draw what I see, and although my artwork will never be in the Measures class, with a few notes, the pictures do come alive. What's more, they are mine, my own personal record, for my own personal use, so does it really matter if they don't stand up to Da Vinci.

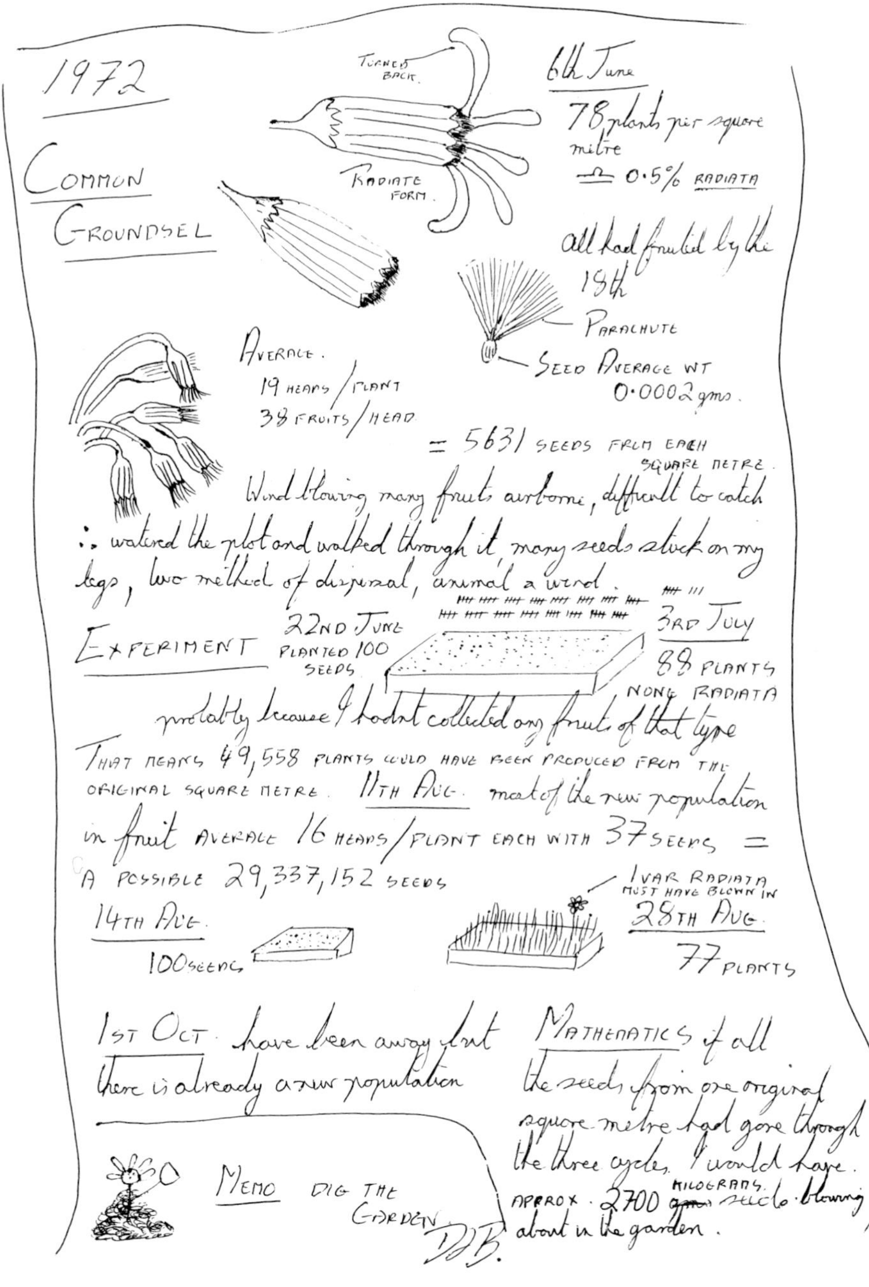

1972

COMMON GROUNDSEL

TURNED BACK

RADIATE FORM.

AVERAGE.
19 HEADS / PLANT
38 FRUITS / HEAD

6th June
78 plants per square metre
0.5% RADIATA

all had fruited by the 18th

PARACHUTE

SEED AVERAGE WT 0.0002 gms.

= 5631 SEEDS FROM EACH SQUARE METRE.

Wind blowing many fruits airborne, difficult to catch ∴ watered the plot and walked through it, many seeds stuck on my legs, two method of dispersal, animal & wind.

EXPERIMENT   22ND JUNE   PLANTED 100 SEEDS

3RD JULY
88 PLANTS
NONE RADIATA

probably because I hadn't collected any fruit of that type

THAT MEANS 49,558 PLANTS WOULD HAVE BEEN PRODUCED FROM THE ORIGINAL SQUARE METRE. 11TH AUG. most of the new population in fruit AVERAGE 16 HEADS / PLANT EACH WITH 37 SEEDS = A POSSIBLE 29,337,152 SEEDS

14TH AUG.
100 SEEDS

1 VAR RADIATA MUST HAVE BLOWN IN
28TH AUG.
77 PLANTS

1ST OCT. have been away but there is already a new population

MATHEMATICS if all the seeds from one original square metre had gone through the three cycles, I would have. APPROX. 2700 KILOGRAMS seeds blowing about in the garden.

MEMO   DIG THE GARDEN
DJB.

Art Nouveau, Bellamy 1972. A weed's a plant growing in the wrong place.

Many of the plants which grow in David's Meadow fall into the category of weeds, but what's a weed? About the best definition I know is that 'a weed is a plant which is growing in the wrong place'. That doesn't help much because all those wonderful plants which grow in our gardens, are, naturally speaking, growing in the wrong place. Mind you my own garden's full of real weeds, and I think that a much better name for them is adventives. That means plants which have the ability to nip in and take advantage of whatever potential there is going. I hope that the page from my diary explains exactly what an adventive is.

From his copious notes David Measures has learned, not only to read but to understand the environment of the insects. He doesn't need a thermometer to measure the temperature, the fact that the Small Copper has just started her daily search for food tells him that the mercury stands above 61°F. He doesn't even need to consult a calender, because it's there flying, buzzing and creeping all around him. The trains which once disturbed the peace of the embankment ran to the strict timetable of the L.M.S. What at first sight looks like a haphazard world of the meadow runs to the even more stringent timetable of the environment. As the tall bridge casts its long shadow down the track, the offspring of that first Wall leaves the warm brickwork to follow the last warmth of day down the evening of the track. David Measures records it all in intricate and exquisite detail. His is total art, an amalgam of the full potential which that environment offers to every living thing, including man.

Interesting as it is to visit David's Meadow, it is of course impossible to go to Southwell without paying a visit to the Cathedral. In fact it is impossible to go anywhere near Southwell without seeing the twin towers which rise above the graceful stone houses that form the heart of the city. I can't quite put my finger on why, but from a distance the dumpy spires which top the towers look out of place, in fact reminding me much more of the Black Forest than the environs of Sherwood. From close quarters the whole thing does, however, blend together. It works, looking as much a part of the scene as if it had grown there. Beautiful as the outside of the building with its time-washed stonework may be, you must go inside to see the real secret of the Minster.

It may take a lot of patience to record and draw the patterns of nature, but think how much more patience would be needed to carve that record in stone. That is just what the stone masons of the 13th century did, for the interior is decorated with many thousands of intricate carvings. There is much evidence to substantiate the fact that the skilled craftsmen who worked in stone travelled the land to any place in which there was work to be done, taking their families and belongings with them. A building the size of a Cathedral, even a mini cathedral like Southwell was a long job. In fact, it took over 200 years to complete and even then bits and pieces were tacked on long after, perhaps even long enough for a number of generations of masons to take in the local scene and soak up a bit of the environment.

The main part of the Minster is decorated in a somewhat formal fashion, as if the artists were using stereotype designs, almost as if they had learned them at some 12th century school of three dimensional art. Please don't get me wrong, I am not trying to run it down; it is absolutely fabulous, delicate, detailed and just right, exactly what the book of Cathedral decoration says there should be. Please go and take a look at the great screen or to give it its right name the pulpitum, which separates the nave from the choir, and look at the choir side where the bulk of the decoration is to be found. If you do, I would like to bet that you will get the urge, to rush out, get a bit of stone and try for yourself. You would not have to go far either to get the real macoy, the actual rock type in which the exquisite carving is executed. It is very close-grained magnesian limestone which was quarried only fifteen miles from the Minster at Mansfield.

The pulpitum, which was completed in about 1350, is however just a taste of what was to come, because something fantastic was happening. By this time the craftsmen and their families must have been accepted Southwellers, and even if they were not they must have been around long enough to be firmly plugged into the local environment. Whether it was this that changed their art form I don't know but, as they started to decorate the chapter house it underwent a radical transformation. Gone is the formality of design, the capitals and arches are decorated with the signs of the Nottinghamshire countryside as it then was, and most famous of all are the Southwell leaves:— Leaves of White Byrony, Hawthorn, Wild Apple and Wild Rose, Tormentil, Buttercup, Oak and Ivy are everywhere, formal in array but exact in detail. These are really living pictures in stone. Some of the acorn cups are full while others are empty but all the detail is there. A cockerel has every feather in place and two dogs still hot from the chase hold a hare in their mouths. The hare looks just dead and the dogs are perfect even to those parts which are hidden from sight at the back of the capital.

My camera, even with notes appended, just didn't do justice to the carvings, so David Measure's wife, Christine, has made a drawing that lives like the original sculpture. Is it a wolf? It could be, because wolves still roamed Britain when Southwell was being built. Is it a dog or something more mythical like a Gryphon, I can't quite make up my mind. There is however no doubt that there is a bunch of grapes in its mouth and to prove it vine leaves are present on other capitals. If it's a Gryphon, then it must be excused as an early example of artistic licence, but the grapes aren't, they are real! Grapes in Nottinghamshire? Yes, up to the early part of the 14th century the vineyards of Britain were famous and these vineyards bore fruits as far north as York.

Vines, hops and mulberries are all woven into the carved frieze, a record of the potential of what was then a much warmer Britain. It's just like a harvest

Detail of Southwell's permanent harvest festival.

festival that has been fresh frozen for more than 600 years.

While we were filming in the Minster the contemporary parishioners were decorating the Church for their own harvest thanksgiving. Many of the fruits of the past were there, blackberries, acorns, hawthorn and apples, but they were admixed with a whole range of exotic fruit, oranges, bananas and lemons; plants which never have grown in these islands of ours.

There in the display, placed almost central in pride of place, was a piece of coal, that product of the earth which, more than all else, has made it possible for us to enjoy the fruits of the whole world.

It was the discovery of the great coalfields (see Chapter 6) that provided the power for the industrial revolution. It was the industrial revolution that opened up our trade potential with the rest of the world and brought an end to our dependence on the fruits of our own immediate landscape.

It is an interesting fact that, not long after the Chapter House was completed, the climate of Britain took a turn for the worse and the vineyards disappeared from England. The record in stone is just one of the many pieces of evidence that tell us of the environment as it was in the 13th century.

It is in this way that, throughout history, the artists have been the librarians of ecological fact, sensing the changing environments and recording them for posterity.

A walk along the corridor that leads to the Chapter House is a walk through this forgotten renaissance; when men turned from their formal art to illustrate the world in which they lived with the care and attention it deserves. After all, it is the only one we have!

Harvest Festival Southwell 1973.

8
SHINGLE, SALT & SILT

The general concensus of opinion is that life began in the sea, in all probability in shallow rock pools at the upper limit of the tide. The argument is that the conditions of concentration and redilution of simple salts which are thought to be necessary for the evolution of living chemicals could have existed in such situations.

The same boundary between the sea and the land still exists today and, somewhat paradoxically, it represents one of the harshest and most extreme habitats for life. Each day for two short periods this zone is immersed in a concentrated solution of salt, or depending on the exact position of the pool the periods of immersion will be at longer intervals during the high spring tides. Between these periods the rock and anything which tries to live there will be exposed to either the full blast of the sun and the icy winds of winter and/or to a downpour of pure distilled rainwater. This is not the perfect habitat for any living organism.

The coasts of the British Isles are picked out by a zone in which very few plants can eke out an existence. The width of the zone varies greatly from a few centimetres in the case of a vertical cliff to several kilometres where the shore slopes almost imperceptably into the water. Nevertheless, wherever and for whatever purpose you go down to the sea you have to cross this line.

Wherever the upper tidal zone consists of suitable solid rock it is marked by a ribbon of brown seaweed, the plant body or thallus of which consists of a thick leathery structure that divides into two equal parts at every branch point. The thalli are channeled and look like a folded tongue. If you are one of those people who can't fold their tongues, and there is a one in three chance that you are, then I suggest you go and find someone who can and ask them to demonstrate exactly what the thallus of *Pelvetia canaliculata* looks like. Not that you need bother, because its habitat will identify it for you, as this is the only seaweed which grows in this narrow zone. It is also the only British seaweed which is said to be poisonous, although I have no first-hand proof of the fact.

Above the *Pelvetia* zone the rocks at first sight look as if they have had a good dose of Torrey Canyon. Closer inspection, however, reveals that the black tide mark is not oil, but a zone which is dominated by a thin crust of black lichens which adhere tightly to the rock surface. This zone is variegated with the greys and even bright orange of other lichens and by two flowering plants,

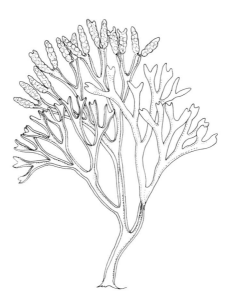

PELVETIA CANALICULATA, hardiest of the seaweeds which grows in a zone of its own.

the neat cushions and pink globe-like heads of the Sea Thrift and the flat-tened rosettes and antler-like leaves of the Stags-horn Plantain.

The harder the substrate, the better developed is the zonation because the one other factor that makes life difficult in the maritime fringe is erosion. Any rock battered by waves and exposed to all the vagaries of the elements will in time be eroded away. The harder the rock, the longer the time taken and hence the more permanent is the habitat. The first stage in the process is the splitting off of lumps of rock forming boulders of various sizes which slide under the force of gravity down into the sea. If you have ever been bathing in a rough sea you will have had personal experience of the next phase of erosion. The boulders are rolled back and forth against the bed rock, in this way they get their corners knocked off, become rounded and eventually wear down to pebble dimensions.

At this stage a really wonderful thing happens. Most of the larger seaweeds, like *Pelvetia*, require solid rock on which to grow in the turbulent surf. How-ever, in the comparative shelter of deeper water, groups of pebbles provide sufficient anchorage for even the great kelps to grow. As the blades of the kelps begin to expand each spring, they act as a bouyant sail and when the area of sail is large enough to overcome the weight of the pebble anchor, the whole ungainly 'ship' starts to move along in the current. Where there are

93

sufficient kelp plants, as the critical phase of growth is reached, the whole forest, together with the attached pebble masses, go leaping along the bottom with a rumble of multiple clicks. The phenomenon of the hopping kelps was first noted by Douglas Hume Wallace, a long standing member of the British Sub Aqua Club, while diving off Selsey Bill. He became so fascinated that since the initial discovery he has spent many hours under water hopping with the pebbles.

His researches have shown that it is a case of 'have kelp will travel' and as long as the plants are in a current they continue their ungainly way along the bottom. Three factors can terminate their journey. During the winter the kelp blades are gradually eroded away and the stipes once again become anchored to the bottom. The journey ends in a similar way if the current moves the 'ship' into deep or dirty water where there is not enough light to sustain growth of the sail. Finally, if the current is inshore the journey will end high and dry on a shingle bank and the twisted stipes of kelps joined to a knot of pebbles are a familiar sight along the strandline in certain areas.

Just how important the kelp pebble flotilla is to the continued build-up of our shingle beaches is still a matter of debate. However, once you have sat on the bottom and witnessed the antics of the leaping armada, it is difficult to imagine that they do not play a significant role. So, wherever there is a good supply of rock, ground to pebble size, kelp and an onshore current, the

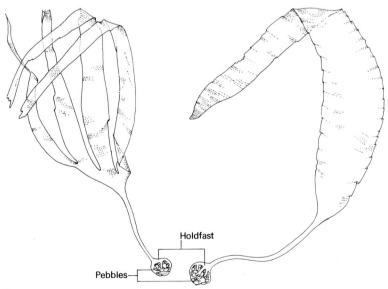

Kelp Yachts.

adjacent coast will be protected by a shingle bank. Two most famous British Banks where the kelp deposits its shingle are the 20 kilometre stretch of Chesil Beach and the great expanse of Dungeness.

If life on solid rock in the upper tidal limit is harsh, then life in the same zone on a pebble beach must be impossible. Added to all the problems of exposure and immersion are the continual effects of grinding, the possibility of premature burial as another kelp boat sheds its load, but above all, the fantastic noise of all those pebbles rubbing together under the force of the waves.

Chesil Bank – how many pebbles are there on this beach?

Pebbles are by definition round pieces of rock. A bucket full of pebbles is in reality only partly full of rock the remainder being filled with space. It is the old problem of packing round apples in a square box. So, even when the pebbles are raised up above the action of the waves, there are still great problems for would-be colonizers. Any rain falling on the surface of the beach will immediately drain through, leaving a dry inhospitable surface. A few plants do, however, manage to use the limited potential for life amongst the pebbles. One is the Maritime Pea whose handsome heads of flowers brighten up the shingle scenes of the south east coast. Another is a much commoner plant, the Goose Grass, which is typically found in hedgerows and wasteland, where it can grow over two metres long and where its numerous 'adhesive' leaves soon make its presence felt. The leaves and round fruits are covered with numerous hooked hairs which act like velcro fasteners and give the plant its other common name, Sticky Willie. Compared with its cousin of the hedgerows, Willie of the shingle banks is a miserable thing which creeps amongst the pebbles. Apart from its size it is exactly like its hedgerow counterpart, simply scaled down to gain survival in the harsh world on the fringe; it is thus best to call it an ecotype.

The rain which falls on the shingle drains down to the lower levels where it forms a hidden reservoir which, although too deep for the plant roots, can be an important source of fresh water for the coastal resorts. On the large wedge of Dungeness, the hidden reservoir surfaces like a series of oases between the ridges of the stony desert. Here other plants manage to get a foothold and an almost lush vegetation of Blackthorn scrub develops, helping further to stabilise the shifting stones. The cracks between the pebbles fill with humus, forming a more fertile soil. Whether, given time the scrub would pass over to forest by the natural process of succession is not known but, one thing the shingle bank has got is time. Unless of course the tide turns and the currents start to carry the shingle back to sea.

While the process of stabilization goes on at the landward side of the bank, the process of building continues on the seaward side. The hopping kelps bring a continuous supply of pebbles to the down current end, often forming a hook like tip to the bank, in the lee of which there is protected water. The exact amount of sea which becomes entrapped behind the shingle bank will of course depend on the position in which the bank starts to form. In the case of Dungeness and Selsey Bill the shingle forms a headland and a minimum of sheltered water is produced. Chesil Beach has, on the other hand, formed across a very shallow bay, cutting off a long sheet of water from the open sea.

It is in such sheltered positions, where the sea still has access at high tide, that the final products of erosion of the rocks may be laid down. Continuous grinding and wave action finally reduces the pebbles to such small dimensions that they are classified as silt. The particles are now too small to serve as

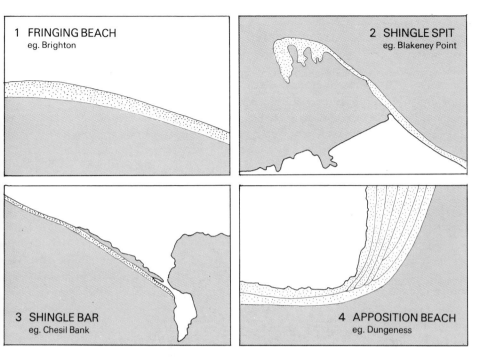

1 FRINGING BEACH eg. Brighton	2 SHINGLE SPIT eg. Blakeney Point
3 SHINGLE BAR eg. Chesil Bank	4 APPOSITION BEACH eg. Dungeness

Types of Shingle Bank

FRINGING BEACH	No protected water.
SHINGLE SPIT	Protected water with salt marshes.
SHINGLE BAR	With sheltered water sometimes tidal sometimes not.
APPOSITION BEACH	No sheltered water. Lines mark the successive banks.

an anchorage for seaweeds and thus the critical factor controlling their further movement is their density. The heavier the particles, the greater will be the amount of water movement necessary to keep them moving, so the finest and lightest will be laid down only in the most sheltered places.

As each tide runs in, round the hook of the shingle bank, it gradually drops its load of suspended material, the finest particles being dropped last at slack water. If nothing further happened the particles would be carried back to sea on the ebb tide; however, here in the muddy hinterland one small plant can grow. This is the Glasswort, *Salicornia* and, unlike the seaweeds, it has roots which grow down into the mud and help to bind it together, holding it fast against the ebbing tide. *Salicornia* is the first colonist which lays down the foundations of new dry land. The easiest way to savour the problems of life for this pioneer is to chew the leaves and taste the salt, for this is one of the few flowering plants which can tolerate the high and variable salinities of the salt

97

marsh environment. *Salicornia* is still collected along the east coast, where it is pickled and sold under the name of Sea Samphire.

Once the Sea Samphire has got a foothold, the process of stabilization is taken over by a group of plants, all of which can tolerate high salinity and all bear the first name Sea; Sea Plantain, Arrow Grass, Milkwort, Aster and Lavender, which together thatch over and stabilise the sticky silts. The whole zone is however still within reach of the high tides and the constant ebb and flow of water maintains sinuous channels which branch, getting smaller and smaller like some complex of blood vessels, feeding and draining the marsh.

If you like splodging, that is, feeling sticky mud oozing between your toes, and I do, then these mud creeks are the ideal places to practise your art. However, care must be taken and the rule is to always splodge en masse, because the mud can be deep and always is tenacious and to get caught on an incoming tide could be catastrophic. Each flood tide comes pouring up the creeks, bringing a new load of silt which overflows on to the marsh flats. As the returning water spills over the lip of the channels it deposits its main load of silt, so that the edges of the waterways are raised into a bank which forms the habitat for one of the largest plants which can grow on the salt marsh *Halimione portulacoides,* the Sea Purslane.

Looking at the beautiful living pattern of the mature salt marsh it is difficult to remember that this is still a very extreme environment for many forms of life. Perhaps, of all the plants which grow and make their home there, the Sea Aster demonstrates this most forceably. On the salt marsh the Sea Aster grows to a height of 10 to 15 centimetres and produces a head of five or six flowers. Transplanted into a well kept garden it will grow to a height of well over one metre with a great plate of its mauve, daisy like flowers. Here is a case of a plant which appears to live way off its optimum habitat. The reason that it does not grow away from the coast, where it would evidently do better, at least in terms of stature and reproductive capacity, is in all probability that it is intolerant of competition with other plants. Why a plant which can tolerate such harsh conditions is intolerant of other plants crowding it, is still a mystery.

Although the cause is too much salt, the main hang up for life on the salt marsh is the availability of water for plant growth. This may appear peculiar because even when the tide is out much of the salt marsh soil remains wet. However, the thing that matters to a plant is not how much water is present in the soil, but whether that water is available for uptake by the plant. Water, once in the silt, is held by a whole complex of forces, one of which is termed the osmotic component and is related to the amount of salts which are bound onto the silt particles, and there's the problem. In order to take up water the plant must overcome these binding forces.

The problem must be especially acute in the salt pans, which are the other main feature of the surface of the higher sections of the marsh. Wherever the silts build up above the range of the daily high tides, water will pond back in any depression for the longer periods of time between the high waters of the spring tide cycle. If no rain falls during this time, the water gradually evaporates, leaving a diamond pattern of cracked mud, topped with a white icing of salt crystals. Little or nothing can live in the salt pans except for stray pieces of Bladderwrack, which roll into tight balls as they grow, and the odd spike of *Salicornia*, which looks like a miniature cactus growing in the parched salt desert.

It is not surprising therefore, that only a few plants are able to grow in the salt marsh environment, and most of these are found wherever silt collects between the tides around our coasts. Many of these have thick, fleshy leaves and not only look like, but must be classified as succulents. The development of succulence is, at least in part, a mechanism for water storage.

The natural patterns of the saltings of Britain are rapidly changing, and it is all due to a second generation visitor from across the Atlantic, a plant that goes under the name of *Spartina X townsendii*. *Spartina maritima* is the latin name for the Cord Grass which grows in estuaries and salt marshes along our coasts. In 1923, a new species of Cord Grass, *Spartina alterniflora* was found growing in Southampton Water, where it got on so well with the local population of English Cord Grass that a new hybrid was soon rampaging up the Solent. The

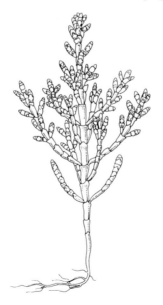

SALICORNIA – Pickled it's called Sea Samphire.

hybrid plant, perhaps due to a mixture of good English stock and new sap from the Americas, was bigger and better in almost every way than either of its parents. So much so that it has ever since progressively taken over our coast, making its relentless way north by both the east and west routes. Such fantastic vigour is often the mark of a hybrid. However, unlike many hybrids which are sterile, and must, therefore, rely on vegetative propagation, *Spartina X townsendii* has produced a fertile race.

Bare tidal mud offers the Cord Grass its optimum habitat; a stray rhizome or seeds acts as an inoculum from whence it grows, often into a perfect circular patch which increases in size until it finally coalesces with an adjacent patch. Thus many square miles of mud are being stabilized each year, adding new dry land to our coastline. If Britain ever does become the nth state of the U.S.A. I feel that our first congressman should be called Townsend in memory of the first American who ruled our coastline, *Spartina X townsendii!* Although X usually marks the spot, in taxonomic parlance it indicates a hybrid.

Anything Spartina can do! Well it is likely that if man can't do better he can at least cash in on the fact. The hybrid Cord Grass has shown that these intertidal muds present great potential to anything that can use them. They are indeed compounded of rocks ground down by the sea, together with material eroded from the land and must, therefore, contain a mixture of all the minerals which are necessary for plant growth. Both the natural salt marsh and the Cord Grass eventually shut off the effects of the tide and, in time, the rain washes out the excess salt from the silty soil, the result being rich pasture land.

All man needs to do is follow the example by building an embankment which is high enough to keep out the highest tide. After drainage, the salt marsh within the embankment can be grazed. Finally, disc harrowing and ploughing completes the job and just 5 years after the last tide was shut out a potato crop can be grown. Silt minus salt, together with the humus, produce rich fertile soil and, what is more, it is dead flat, the perfect place for mechanized farming.

This method of land grabbing was developed by the Dutch, who probably own more tidal silts than any other nation on earth. The technique is called empolderment. Along the coast of Lincolnshire similar flat landscape fringed with salt marshes offers the same potential. Here polders are being constructed and the new soils are carrying a rich harvest of potatoes – one million bags of crisps to the acre! The only problem is that you have to add salt because the salt marsh silts have in the process lost their savour.

The rather sobering fact is that behind the new embankments there are old ones which were constructed by the Romans, and beyond the new sea defences the natural process of deposition and accretion goes on; adding new potential to the realm of shingle, salt and silt.

9
A WALK THROUGH THE HILLS

You don't have to go to Africa or up the Amazon to make surprising discoveries; the countryside of Britain is full of 'em and, nowhere more so than the Isle of Purbeck. For your next Safari, how about Darkest Dorset? The best route of discovery is to follow the hills from Kimmeridge, north by east, to Corfe Castle and then on to Poole Harbour. A total journey, as the pterodactyl flew, of only ten miles; yet in this short distance you will travel over no less than six different rock types, each of which supports a different type of vegetation. In these few miles you will also have walked (or to take a leaf out of Mr. Spock's log-book, warped), through 150 million years of geological time. If you want visual proof, well, there's a quarry not far from Swanage in which you can get an uneasy feeling that you are back in the age of the Dinosaurs. It was here that the quarrymen uncovered a series of giant tracks made up of large, three toed, clawed footprints; and the feet that made them belonged to a Dinosaur probably a Megalosaurus.

With the great revival of 'monster' films: GODZILLA, KING KONG, GORGO I get the feeling that, one night, the Purbeck picturegoers could be in for a shock on their way home after two hours of BINGO, which seems to be the latest 'monster horror' showing at most of the local cinemas.

The quarry owner was not in search of footprints; what he wanted was the famous Portland Stone, which is such high class rock that it was used in the construction of the Bank of England and many of the other more affluent manmarks of Britain. Down he went, through the overlying Purbeck Stone and then he struck it rich! He came to the stratum which bore the marks of the Megalosaurus. Fantastic as the discovery was, it must have become a bit of an embarrassment because all the 'dinosaurologists' wanted to see, photograph and measure them. Here was a chance to find out how these giants of the past walked, a chance actually to measure their ungainly gait.

So quarrying was held up while the essential work was completed and then the blocks of stone, each with its precious print, were lifted and taken to adorn the walls of museums.

I must put in a plea for always paying a visit to the local museum. Wherever you go on holiday in Britain there will be one nearby; don't leave it to that rainy day that may never come. The local museum should be your first stop and I guarantee that even a quick look round will help to make your holiday

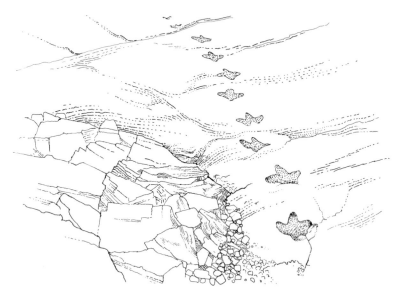

A nightmare after Bingo. Footprint of a Megalosaurus not far from Swanage.

come alive. There is a fantastic one at Dorchester, where you can measure yourself up against the great three-toed prints.

The quarry in question was on one side of a hill and, surprise! surprise! or so the story goes, another quarryman, on the other side of the hill, struck the same stratum and the continuation of these same tracks were there – trotting out on his side. So it has gone on, more footprints being found in other quarries. Evidently, and the evidence is pretty concrete, there was a whole herd of dinosaurs out for their afternoon stroll on the swampy edge of the lagoon in which this sheet of rock was being laid down. What probably happened was that the next tide brought in more than its fair share of mud, filling and preserving the tracks, which did not again see the light of day for 140 million years. The Megalosaurus in question either walked straight through the hill, or the rocks which form the upper part of the hill were not there at the time. We know the latter to be the case and we also know that it took its walk at a very impressionable stage.

Have you ever wondered how map-makers made maps, especially before the advent of aerial photography? Now that we have this rapid method of spot-checking, it is surprising to find how accurate some of the early cartographers were. They worked solely on the basis of what they could see as they tramped our countryside and their eye for detail can only be described as phenomenal. Geological cartographers, even when supplied with aerial photographs, are batting on an even rockier wicket, because they only rarely can see

102

the strata which they are mapping. The rocks lie hidden either by soil or vegetation, usually both. Mind you, each of these gives clues as to what lies underneath because they are in reality all part of the same system.

The corner stones of geological mapping are, however, the natural rock outcrops along the coasts and river valleys. The man-made cliffs in quarries and cuttings are also of great help because, in such places, it is easy to see what strata are present and which way they are lying; over the rest of the area, the soils get in the way.

Imagine what would happen if the floor of the footprint quarry were left for a very long time undisturbed by man, but open to the vagaries of wind and weather. The bare rock, crisscrossed with the tracks and with cracks, both natural and man-made, would gradually be broken down by the action of frost and rain. This natural process of breakdown is called 'weathering'. The rock surface is thus made more hospitable for the growth of plants and colonisation of the surface gets underway. Once plants are present, their roots will speed up the process of rock breaking (remember the power of the oak seedling when it comes to lifting tombstones!) and begins to add humus to the crumbling rock. Leaves falling on to the surface are potential food for animals and so the soil soon becomes inhabited by worms and insects; all of which, unlike plants, move about. This movement helps to keep the whole thing well stirred, speeding up the process of soil formation or pedogenisis. ROCK + PLANTS + ANIMALS + TIME = SOIL = LIVING SOIL.

As the weathering works deeper and deeper into what was solid rock, the rain carries minerals and humic substances down through the developing profile which eventually becomes layered. The final product is a mature, layered soil study of the structure, which can tell you a lot about its fertility. One good reason for going and watching someone else dig a hole is to look at the structure of the soil. The drawing on page 104 shows the main layers which may be found in a mature soil and that on page 105 the main types found in the Isle of Purbeck. Each one differs in structure, proportions of the various minerals present, porosity to water and, of course, fertility.

Fertility is a difficult concept to use; the farmer knows what he means by a fertile soil, but his definition relates only to the crops he tries to grow in that soil. As far as the natural vegetation is concerned, each is fertile enough for the vegetation which grows on it, because that vegetation has evolved to thrive on that particular soil. This is the essence of evolution, the development of structured living systems, all components of which together, reap the potential of the environmental cocktail.

So it is easy to see that a soil is a structured living entity, an amalgam of the parent rock, the flora, the fauna and the climate; a working unit which is the foundation of our living landscapes. With this basic information and without the power of our mythical Megalosaurus, it is possible to take a walk through

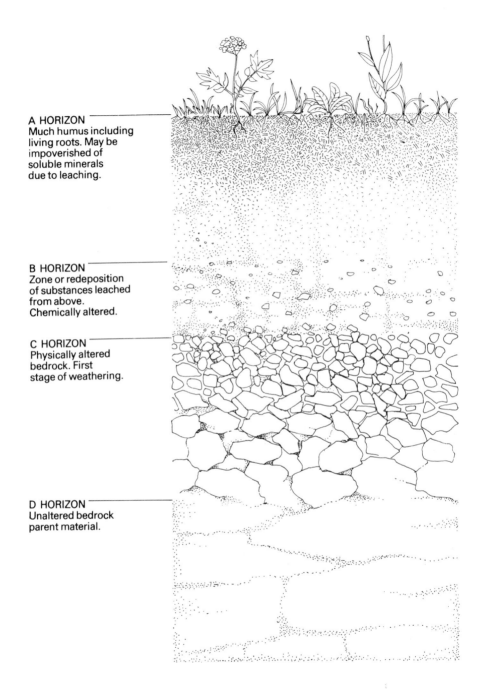

A HORIZON
Much humus including
living roots. May be
impoverished of
soluble minerals
due to leaching.

B HORIZON
Zone or redeposition
of substances leached
from above.
Chemically altered.

C HORIZON
Physically altered
bedrock. First
stage of weathering.

D HORIZON
Unaltered bedrock
parent material.

The profile of mature soil.

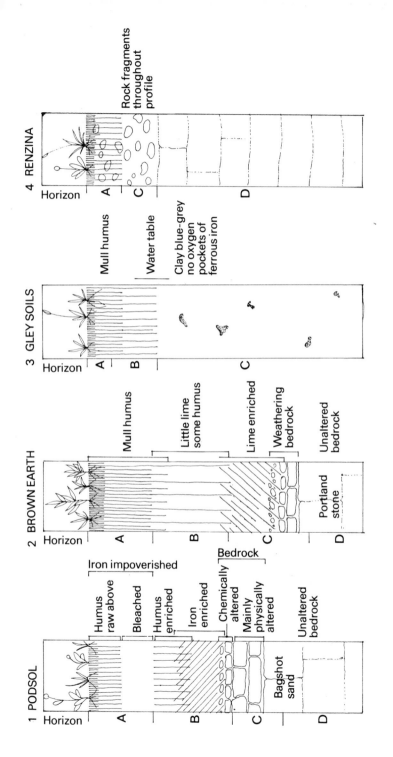

Main soil types found on the Isle of Purbeck

1. PODSOL with iron humus hard pan, formed from Bagshot Sand – *Heathland.*
2. BROWN EARTH formed from portland beds, also where clays and sands are mixed – *Well drained good arable soil.*
3. GLEY SOILS formed from both Wealden and Kimmeridgee clays. (Horizon absent being replaced by the blue grey or gley horizon – *Heavy poorly drained soils meadowland.*)
4. RENZINA formed from Purbeck stone and chalk. Shallow soils, well to excessively drained, rock fragments to the surface – *Arable soils.*

the hills and do a bit of instant geology en-route.

At the coast it is all too easy. The tall cliffs hide no secrets. It is, in fact, as clear as mud because Kimmeridge Bay gives its name to the bedrock, Kimmeridge clay. Here, close to the sea, it is difficult to get away from it, especially in wet weather. It is also difficult to get away from the large fossil shells which abound in the cliffs. Just about everywhere you look along this stretch of coast, there are remains of ammonites. Ammonites are the shells of large octopus-like creatures which must have been abundant off the coast of Purbeck in the Jurassic times. The soft parts of the animal lived in the terminal chamber of the shell and its legs poked out for feeding and when moving about. Looking at a modern day octopus or squid, it is very difficult to realise that they are Molluscs, that is, they are related to snails. The ammonites are the missing link, at least for the disbelievers. The older specimens must have found their protective houses very unwieldy because, safe in their shells, they grew to enormous sizes; shells more than one metre across being not uncommon.

The great reptiles lived at the same time as the ammonites and there is evidence that some of them lived a semi-aquatic life, letting the buoyant

An ammonite.

106

water support at least part of their weight. I can't help wondering what happened if a dinosaur ever sat down to rest on an ammonite! Was the shell dinosaur-proof?

Whether such a saga ever did occur we shall never know; what we do know is that the bulk of the Kimmeridge clays were laid down in the sea and in relatively deep water, so it is unlikely to have happened during the time this particular strata was being deposited. We also know that the sea level was falling and/or the land level was rising, which, in the long run, amounts to the same thing. We know this because the next lot of rock laid down on top of the clay was of a very different sort; not a deep-water clay but shallow-water sands and limestones, the Portland and Purbeck beds.

It is easy to pick out the areas in which the Kimmeridge clay comes to the surface because they are covered with dense, wet scrub and woodlands made up of willow and alder. The wet, heavy clay soils differ markedly from the well-drained neutral to slightly acid soils derived from the Portland stone and the red-brown calcareous soils formed from the Purbeck limestones. Both the latter soils are well drained and produce good arable land, so there is little or no natural vegetation left in this area. All evidence indicates that they were originally covered in mixed, deciduous woodland.

The Portland and Purbeck beds are both sedimentary rocks; that is, they were laid down as sediments in water. The evidence indicates that they were formed in the shallow water of lagoons, the presence of ammonites being enough proof that conditions were still marine. However, the youngest of the Purbeck limestones are full of shells which have a distinct fresh-water flavour about them. These were laid down about 15 million years after the Kimmeridge clays. In this 15 million years, the sea had gone from the area and fresh-water conditions prevailed, at least while the Upper Purbeck beds were deposited. The succession of sedimentary rocks is thus a record of environmental change brought about by a change in sea level.

This was, however, just the beginning of the story of change, because the sea water returned and the next strata, which were deposited only 100 million years ago were the famous Wealden clays which generations of gardeners have grumbled about. It is interesting to note that we do not have to specify B.C. or B.P. (before present) because what's an odd 2000 years when you are talking about millions. The whole of *anno domini* is less than 0·005% of the time since our Megalosaurus went walkies. It all makes me feel quite young!

It is possible to stand on high ground of the coastal hills and look out across to the well drained soils which cover the chalk ridge. Most prominent is Corfe Castle, which stands on its peculiar island of chalk between two gaps in the escarpment. Between the outcrops of the Purbecks and the Chalk is the broad tract of Wealden clay.

Clay is a remarkable substance, consisting of a number of very special

107

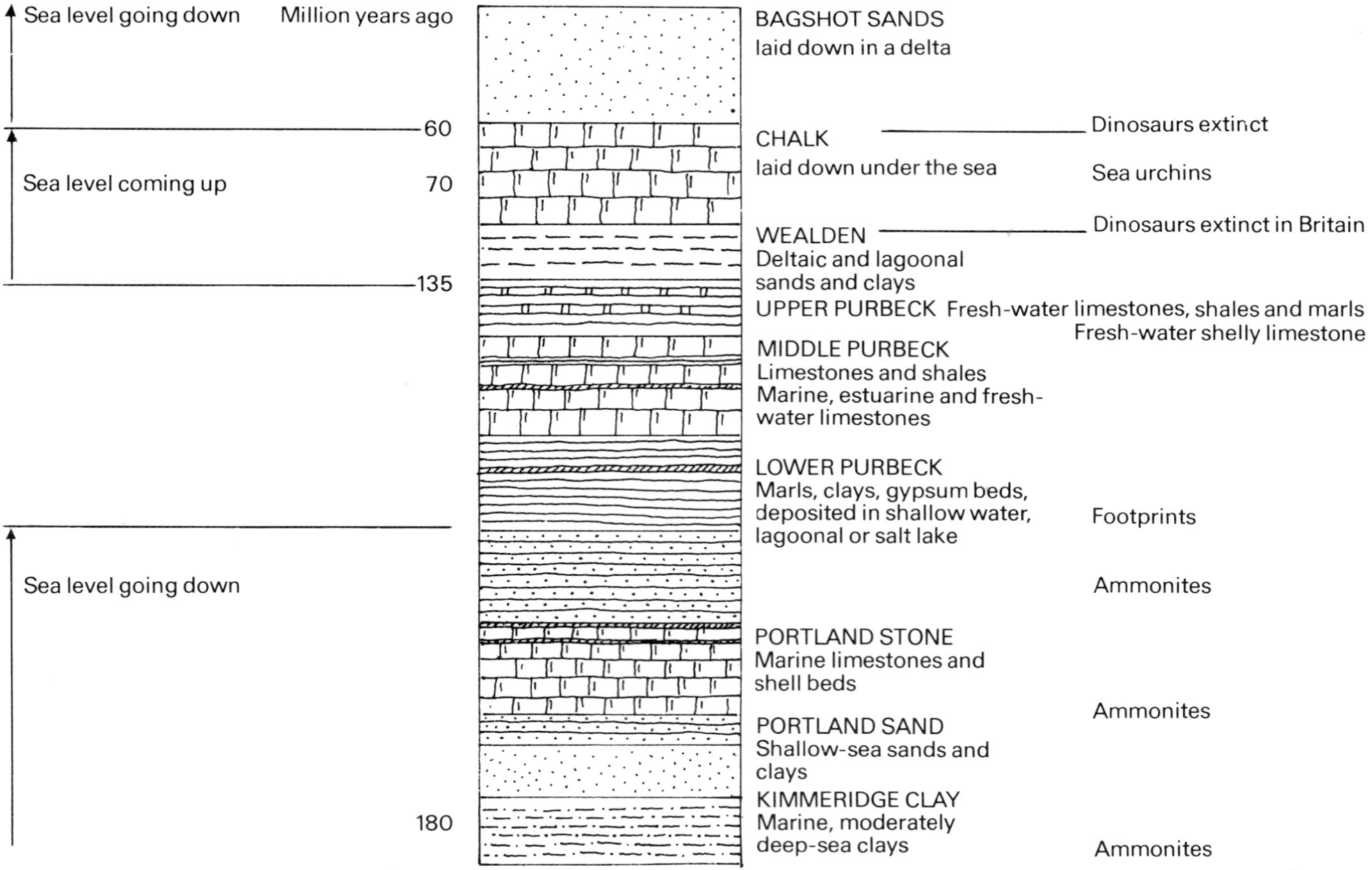

Million years ago		

Sea level going down

BAGSHOT SANDS — laid down in a delta

Dinosaurs extinct

— 60 —

Sea level coming up

CHALK — laid down under the sea

Sea urchins

— 70 —

WEALDEN — Deltaic and lagoonal sands and clays — Dinosaurs extinct in Britain

UPPER PURBECK — Fresh-water limestones, shales and marls / Fresh-water shelly limestone

— 135 —

MIDDLE PURBECK — Limestones and shales. Marine, estuarine and fresh-water limestones

LOWER PURBECK — Marls, clays, gypsum beds, deposited in shallow water, lagoonal or salt lake — Footprints

Sea level going down

PORTLAND STONE — Marine limestones and shell beds — Ammonites

PORTLAND SAND — Shallow-sea sands and clays — Ammonites

— 180 —

KIMMERIDGE CLAY — Marine, moderately deep-sea clays — Ammonites

A column of sedimentary rock is a record of the environmental history of the age in which it was laid down.

108

minerals which have a marked capacity for hanging on to things! The clay minerals, which are formed during the process of weathering, are therefore of great importance in the formation of a structured soil, helping to bind the mineral particles together to form those all important soil crumbs. However, you can always have too much, even of a good thing and too much clay produces too much structure, the result is a heavy brick wall of a soil which impedes drainage. Nevertheless, most of the Wealden clay in the area has been put to plough or is under good pasture but, wherever it is left untended there is the tell-tale Willow and Alder.

One area in the middle of the Weald clay stands out like a sore thumb. Here the clay is admixed with a lot of sand and here on Corfe Common rough grazing land of grass heath predominates. Here too we must leave the friendly dinosaur because, by the time that the next strata were laid down, the dinosaurs were probably extinct, at least in Britain. They certainly walked the Wealden clay, in fact the first dinosaur remains were found in the Wealden clay at Whitemans Green in Sussex, only 150 years ago by a certain gentleman named Gideon Algernon Mantell. In other parts of the world they appear to have lasted a bit longer; but by 65 million years ago they were all extinct. It is one of those time honoured misconceptions that early man hunted with the dinosaurs. This is untrue; these great reptiles were extinct long before man was ever 'thought of'.

The Chalk is the most conspicuous of all the strata in the Isle of Purbeck and the grey-white soils, which are well drained and rich in lime, are mostly under arable crops. However, the steeper, unploughable slopes are given over to grazing land which is in reality a westward extension of the chalk downs of Sussex and Kent.

At the base of the steep slopes, where rubble, eroded from the escarpment, has collected, the scrubby vegetation of ash is often dominated by stinging nettles, which form a good first line of defence against all would-be scalers of the heights of Corfe Castle. The little bumps which come up on your skin are the result of an allergic reaction to a complex substance produced by the stinging cells that adorn the leaf.

Fortunately the area is well supplied with Dock, the leaves of which can cure the burning pain at a rub. Around Corfe Castle the common Broad Leaved Dock grows in abundance but, mixed with it, is the much more uncommon Fiddle Dock. This is one of the plants which is best labelled as a 'southerner' as it is found only south of that imaginary line which joins the Humber to the Severn. It is very easy to recognise, having branches which stand out almost at right angles to the stem so that, when in fruit, the whole thing forms a complex entangled mass. The leaves are, to use the proper term, panduriform, which means that they are shaped like the back of a violin; hence the common name of this plant. The problem is that some of the other

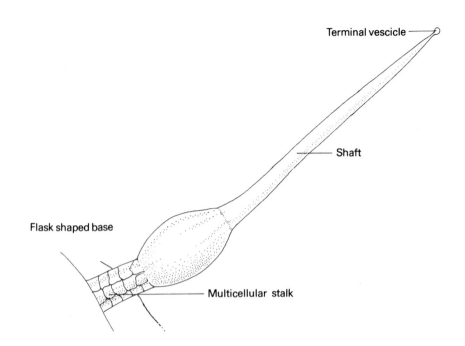

Terminal vescicle

Shaft

Flask shaped base

Multicellular stalk

The stinging nettle URTICA DIOICA (it wasn't called urtica because it urts). The terminal vesicle breaks off on contact injecting a drop of liquid.

docks can have panduriform leaves, so the only way to be sure that you have the Fiddle Dock is to look at the great mass of branches. By the way, when it comes to curing nettle stings, it works just as well as the common dock.

Corfe Castle forms a good vantage point from which to 'recce' the route to the north east. Not far away in the direction of Poole Harbour the scenery changes abruptly; the downlands and the grey-white fields being replaced by sandy soils which support heathland and bog. It is an interesting illusion, since from a distance the paths across the dry, sandy heaths look like continuations of the white chalk. The reason is that here the 800 millimetres of rain each year has leached most of the minerals out of the nutrient-poor sands and along the paths where there is no vegetation, there is no humus to give colour to the sand.

The heathland soils are 'podsols' which are perhaps one of the most typical types of soil to be found in our wet Atlantic climate. Podsols are characterised by excessive leaching of the upper layers; the leached minerals and humic compounds being deposited lower in the soil as a hard layer which is called a 'pan'. The pan is often rich in iron compounds and is so hard that it forms a barrier, both to the penetration of roots and to the drainage of water. The presence of the hard pan inhibits the deep percolation of drainage waters so that most of the small valleys are waterlogged and are filled with peat. Peat

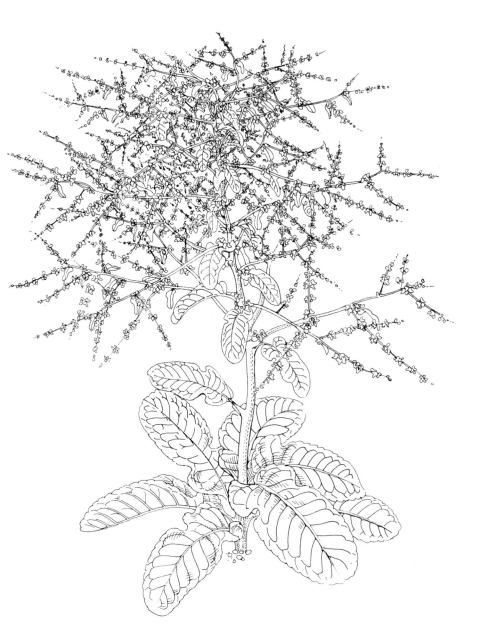

The Fiddle Dock – Rumex pulcher.

111

may be regarded as the youngest form of 'bedrock' as it is still in the process of formation.

These acid sands were laid down a mere 60 million years ago and they take their name, the Bagshot sands, from their type locality in Surrey. All the evidence goes to indicate that the Bagshot sands of the Isle of Purbeck, in fact of the whole of the Hampshire Basin, were laid down in fresh water, probably in the delta of some great river. Thus it would seem that, after deposition of the chalk, the sea level once again fell.

All rock types in the area must, therefore, be classed as sedimentary, except for the peat which is hardly classifiable as rock at all; yet again this is being formed under water. The Peat began to form, at the earliest, some 8000 years B.C. (and note, we must now designate the point of reference, because 1974 years is quite an appreciable slice of 8000 years) and in some of the valleys it is still being formed. The small, wet, peaty areas are best called valley mires and they are common features throughout the area of the Bagshot sands, being especially well developed around the area of Poole Harbour. From the air, each valley mire looks not unlike a glacier which fills the valley and is 'flowing' downhill, rather like a great, elongated drop of one of those thixotropic paints.

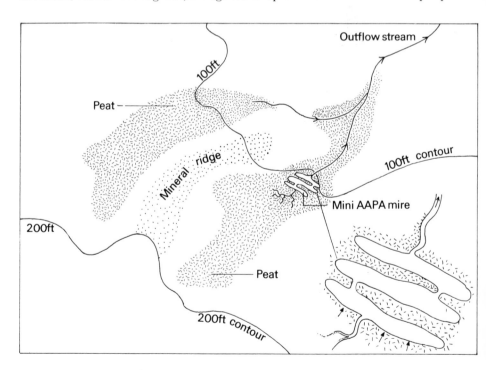

A mini aapamire from the Isle of Purbeck.

It isn't just an illusion because, in places where the angle of slope of the valley floor is sufficient, the semi-liquid peat mass is actually on the move, flowing downhill very very slowly. Wherever it is moving too fast for the new growth of peat to keep pace with it, the surface tears and splits, and elongated pools result, which run at right angles to the slope. From the air, these sections of the mire are very distinct and should be called 'Aapa Mires'. Aapa is a Scandinavian word which means a mire, with a surface which consists of elongate pools separated by long hummocks of living peat, which run at right angles to the slope of the mire. The Scandinavians need a special word in their language for this type of mire, because very large areas of both Finland and Sweden are covered by aapamire. So these tiny aapamires of Purbeck do not make very good signposts. However, a good look round would soon tell you that you are not in Fennoscandia.

Some of the valley mires show another very interesting phenomenon which really does indicate how quite small differences in the environment can have profound effects on the vegetation. In some of the mire systems, sufficient water flows into the valley to form a central stream. This is especially well shown by the valley mires of the New Forest region, which is not far away on the other side of Poole Harbour. These small valleys with their central streams represent a zoned environment and each zone is characterised by its own particular vegetation.

Close to the central stream, where perhaps a little more nutrient is brought in and where the constant flow of water must carry away some of the acid products of the plants that live there, the water is only slightly acid and willow and alder can thrive. These elongate strips of gallery forest are rich in plants and are excellent places in which the wildlife of the surrounding open heath can find shelter.

Passing out from the forest, water flow is more impeded and the waters and the peats become gradually more acid, as the Bog Moss, *Sphagnum*, takes over dominance. To be able to appreciate the subtle changes of the vegetation, it is necessary to be a good field botanist, because the majority of the indicators are quite small mosses some of which like the *Sphagna*, are very difficult to tell apart. However, two readily recognisable plants do pick out the zonation pretty well. The Bog Myrtle and the Common Reed both grow in abundance in certain places. Close to the central strip of forest both grow tall and robust, but they get progressively more stunted towards the edge of the valley. As they get smaller, the Cross Leaved Heath becomes gradually more abundant until, at the edge of the mire proper, it takes over dominance in the wet heath which fringes the peat mass. Passing up the side of the valley, which may be a rise of only a few centimetres, the seepage lines are left behind and heather takes over dominance from the Cross Leaved Heath.

These heaths and mires are not only sanctuaries for a whole range of plant

H

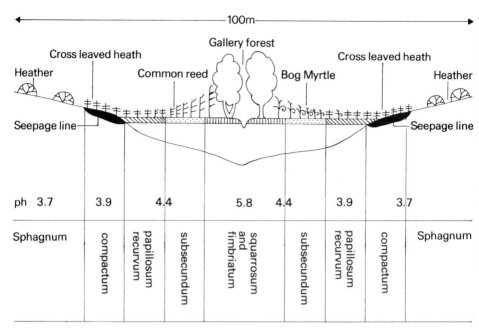

A valley mire, each zone representing a different potential to the evolution of vegetation.

and animal life, but are themselves very special. Each one is a natural system which has evolved to make use of the meagre potential of the acid soils of the Bagshot sands. Each zoned valley mire system with its adjacent heaths is a working unit of evolution, each facet of which makes its own particular use of the environments of the valley and leaves its own special mark on the landscape.

Unfortunately, the heathlands of this region are in retreat; land is precious and many types of development, agricultural, housing, industrial, etc. are taking their yearly toll. Fortunately, some of the best areas are now preserved for posterity as nature reserves of one type or another. The gradual erosion of the heathlands which are left is still, however of great concern, for as each piece is lost, a piece of the information which relates to the evolution of these systems is gone for ever.

So, the Isle of Purbeck is a very special part of Britain, mainly because of the great variety of rock types that outcrop over a very small area. Each offers a different potential both to nature and to man.

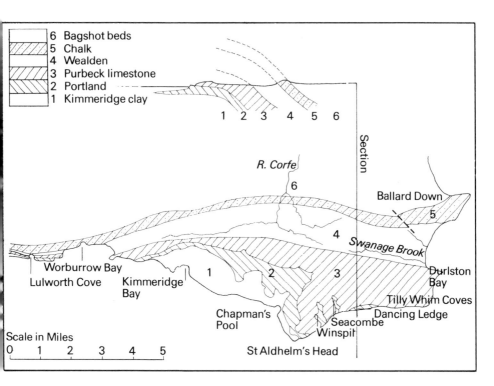

Key:
6 Bagshot beds
5 Chalk
4 Wealden
3 Purbeck limestone
2 Portland
1 Kimmeridge clay

The diversity of rock types exposed on the Isle of Purbeck.

10
IT ALL COMES OUT
IN THE WASH

In the early part of the 17th century, fourteen London businessmen founded a company called the Gentlemen Adventurers. Their aim was to conquer the age-old enemies of the Angles namely too much water and too few hills.

Certain parts of East Anglia and Lincolnshire, especially those bordering on the Wash are as flat as the proverbial pancake, and although the area receives only about 700 millimetres of rain each year, it is a very wet place, at least underfoot. The Gentlemen Adventurers thus set themselves a formidable task, a task which had vanquished many before them, including the skills of the Roman Army.

It was the Romans who drove Car Dyke from Lincoln to Ramsay and then out towards the Wash. It is still there today laid out with military precision, another mark of their skill as civilizing engineers; yet it had little effect on the watery world of weeds and wildfowl. The Great Fenland remained a barrier to progress. The crux of the problem is that you can stand immersed, many miles from the sea, in the middle of this great morass, and although your head is clear of the water, your feet are at, or even below, sea level. So, if the fens were to be drained, the water had to be lifted up so that it could flow out to the sea.

Many, like the Romans, tried and failed, until the Gentlemen Adventurers imported a Dutch engineer by the name of Cornelius Vermuyden to help plan the job. Vermuyden brought the know-how from the similar flat landscape of Holland, not far away on the other side of the North Sea. He planned the construction of the great dykes, embanking them in places more than five metres above the flat terrain. He planned the windpumps to lift the water into them.

It is funny that we tend to think of globe trotting engineers and environmental trouble shooters as very modern things. We also think that local pressure groups who actively lobby against changes in their environment are a syndrome of the second half of the 20th century. Nothing of the sort – the local people who walked the fens on tall stilts, making their living from wild-fowl and fish, really stirred up the local aggro. STILTWALKER OK! CLOGGIES OUT!

Despite the protests, the work went ahead and very gradually the 2500 square miles began to dry out and some of the world's best farm soils came into existence. The origin of this richness lay in the chalk hills which form the

116

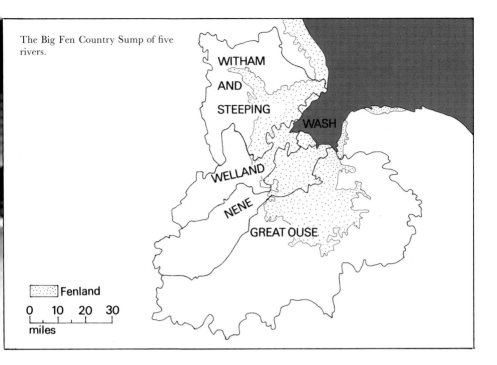

The Big Fen Country Sump of five rivers.

WITHAM

AND

STEEPING

WASH

WELLAND

NENE

GREAT OUSE

Fenland

0   10   20   30
miles

south eastern perimeter of the fens and the clay covered limestones to the west. The headwaters of the rivers Cam, Ouse, Nene and Welland eroding back into the soft strata carried a constant supply of lime and other nutrients down towards the flatlands of the coast. It was these nutrients which nurtured the dense fen vegetation, part of which was locked up in the rich fen peats. The fen peats were laid down gradually, building the landscape up above the present day sea level. During much of the period of the formation of the fens the sea level was much lower. The world was recovering (and maybe it still is) from the effects of the last ice age which, at its maximum, lowered the oceans by about one hundred metres. With all these changes taking place, it is almost impossible to guess exactly what the Wash looked like when the fens reigned supreme.

The dykes were constructed, the windpumps turned and gradually the waters retreated, opening up the enormous potential to man. It was not easy, in fact it was a long slow downhill struggle, which was to take more than two hundred years to complete.

Today there are still many problems, not the least being the fact that drainage not only opens up the potential to man, but opens up the fertile fen soils to the air and to the process of decay. Once drained the rich fen soil, which was

117

laid down over thousands of years, is a wasting asset and in places it is wasting away very rapidly. Thus we have a real problem. The level of the North Sea is still coming up and wastage is taking the level of the fen soils down to meet (in some places to below), the high tide mark. The whole business of keeping the fens drained thus becomes more problematical, high walls now hold the sea at bay and more lifting power is needed to get the water up and out. Despite all precautions, on a number of occasions the wrong combination of high tide and onshore wind has ended in the catastrophe of extensive flooding. However, even the floods can have a beneficial effect as with the sea water comes silt to bolster up the dwindling soils.

Before I had tried it, I used to think how terrible it would be to live in the flat lands, to me hills made landscapes. Having spent quite a lot of time in the big peat country I have changed my mind. There a bicycle gives you the freedom of real horizons, the same freedom that you get when out to sea, and with it comes the realisation that the world isn't flat. A fenland sunset is a sight never to be forgotten, but best of all is an electric storm driving across the fens, or the full arc of the rainbow that follows in its wake.

One centre of the fenland is King's Lynn and the centre of King's Lynn, especially the area around the customs house, is very like parts of Old Amsterdam. Both landscapes have moulded man's activities along the same lines even as far as their architecture. It was here in the market that elvers, baskets made from osiers (which is a local name for the willow *Salix viminalis*) and goosefeathers, all gleaned from the fen, were the articles of commerce. Today the market is in good straight carrots, regimented onions and bulbs that bulge with promise, the modern produce of the rich peat soils.

It was the Gentlemen Adventurers who saw the possibilities; it was Vermuyden fresh from the flat landscapes of Holland who had the environmental know-how to put their dreams into practice. He came, he saw familiar sights, he conquered the flatlands and, what is more, he got knighted for the job he did. When I think of all that wonderland of rustling reeds, water and wildfowl, I can't help wishing that he had stayed at home. Mind you I must confess that I say that through a good mouthful of superb Lincolnshire carrots!

On the borders of Norfolk and Suffolk there's one spot on the B111 road near the village of Garboldisham (pronounced Garblesham), where you can stand on, what must be, the flattest watershed in Britain. To the west of the road the Little Ouse gathers its waters from a morass of alder woods, to flow north through what was part of the Great Fen to enter the Wash at King's Lynn. To the east of the road a series of springs seep up after rain to feed the River Waveney which flows to Lowestoft and the North Sea.

It was in the valleys of the Waveney, the Yare and the Bure that another group of 'industrialists' had been hard at work throughout the middle ages

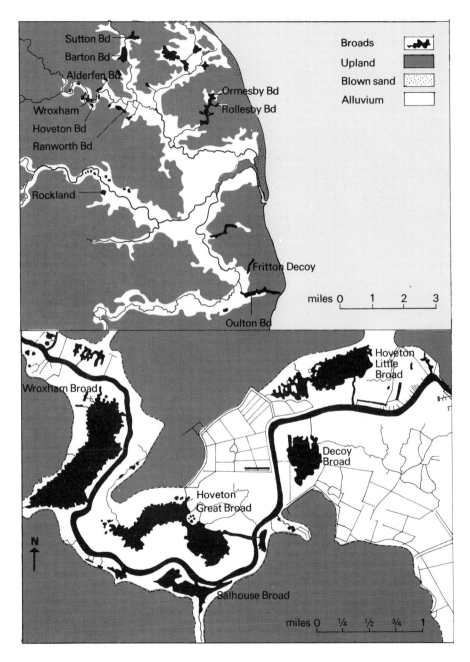

Top map, The Broads, all that's left of the Great Peat Industry of the Middle Ages.
The lower map is just to prove that rivers go round not through Broads.

119

dealing with another lot of fens. This was, throughout the middle ages, one of the more affluent and peopled parts of England, there being 65 persons to the square mile in the 14th century. It was also, according to Domesday statistics, almost devoid of woodlands and in those days no wood meant no fires. The locals thus turned to the fen peat which filled the flat wide river valleys and began to dig great pits from which they won their fuel and their rights of turbary. Their industry must have been enormous and yet it was soon forgotten, their peat quarries were left to fill with water and in time they came to be known as the Norfolk Broads.

There's only one way to see the Broads and that from the deck of a Wherry. Wherries weren't designed to do their job, but rather evolved, to be the work horses of this windswept world. What was needed was a boat which could carry bulk cargoes of sand, gravel and the like along the shallow, often narrow, always winding rivers, and sail close hauled to the wind down the long straight dykes. What is more, they had to be got through the low bridges of Broadland handled by a crew which could be as small as one man and a boy. They didn't get the design right at the first attempt, but in time everything clicked into its right place and the first real Wherry graced the Broads. What is more the Wherry went on evolving and the *Albion,* which sadly is the only one left in

The Albion, last of the Black Sailed Traders. A wherry nice way to travel the Broads.

120

original working trim, was carvel built to be just 4 inches slimmer in the beam so that she could slip through the locks and thus 'pinch' the trade up beyond Bungay.

It was Arthur Ransomes book, Coot Club, which first introduced me to the Broads and left me with a burning desire to take a Wherry through the infamous bridge at Potter Higham, which is the smallest of all the navigable bridges. While we were making the film that goes with this chapter I got my chance. The trouble is that now I'm hooked on the slap slap of the water wherrying under the forefoot of the *Albion,* and the power of the black canvas sail which stretches halfway to heaven and most of the way across the broadland dykes, bringing fear into the fibre glass hearts of the pleasure boats. Even the sail of a Wherry is something of a legend. The new sails are as white as the halyards are wicked, their job being to catch the wind and keep the Wherry at work. It may be all very well to stow the sails of a tarted up pleasure boat, not so the wherry's sails they stay out loose rolled in all weathers. In order to stop them from rotting, the sails were oiled and so, slowly they became blacker and blacker, giving the Wherries their other name of the Black Sailed Traders. Next time you take to the Broads keep a look out for *Albion* and go and take a long sad look at the hulks of wherries past, which just stand proud of the water at the entrance to Ranworth Broad.

The fascination of the Broads, especially to the sailor, is the mixture of environments in which to test his many skills, like the tidal waters of Breydon and Great Yarmouth, where a wrong decision, even slight hesitation on the tiller, could lead to disaster. Then there are the meanders of the natural rivers, where each turn brings a new challenge to be run with or tacked against, or the straight man-made dykes, where, if the wind is in the wrong direction, the weak-hearted turn to engine power, while the real environmentalists unship the long quant and work their passage up to the Broad. Each Broad has a character all of its own, although each is edged in part by reedswamp, fen and carr. Carr is a special name for fen woodland dominated by alder and willow in which the two Buckthorns are often found growing. The purging Buckthorn, *Rhamnus catharticus*, which is armed with sharp thorns has a green fruit which turns black when ripe. *Frangula alnus,* the Alder Buckthorn which, although armed with an emetic, is devoid of thorns has a more flamboyant fruit which ripens from green through red to violet black.

My favourite Broads are the Ormesby, Filby and Rollesby complex which lie at the head of the chocked Muck Fleet which helps to protect their secrets. This brings us on to one very peculiar fact and that is that you can sail the Broadland rivers and never sail through a Broad. If you want to sail the open water then a detour is necessary. That's what makes the Broads different. Rivers flow through lakes, but they flow alongside the Broads and thereby hangs one of the most fascinating tales ever unravelled in the annals of ecology.

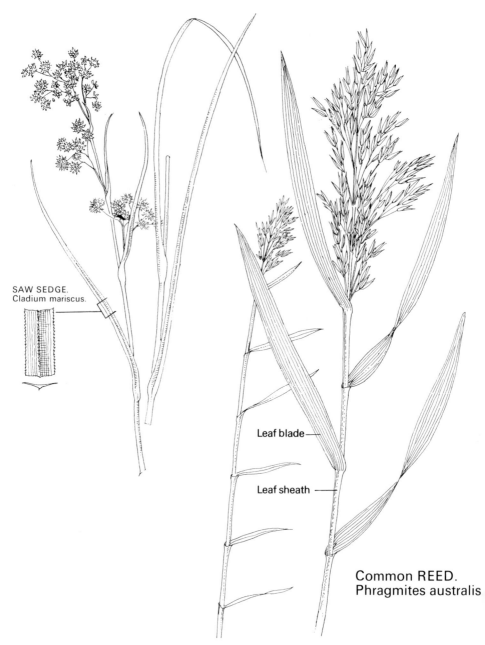

SAW SEDGE.
Cladium mariscus.

Leaf blade

Leaf sheath

Common REED.
Phragmites australis

Dominant plants of Broadland.

122

For whatever reason one looks at the Broads, it is difficult to think that they are not completely natural lakes which are gradually being filled in with peat as the aquatic plants invade the open water. The majority of the plants which are now choking and filling the Broads are the same species which produced the peat of the Great Fen and one of the most typical is the Saw Sedge, *Cladium mariscus*. The large golden brown flower heads immediately belie its presence, but this plant is easily identified on a dark night with your eyes shut, all you need to do is walk through it, it is a lacerating experience. The Saw Sedge is a very vigorous plant, so much so that little or nothing grows in amongst it. However, if the sedge (that is a local name used to describe vegetation dominated by this plant), is mown each year, the whole character of the vegetation soon changes. Cladium loses its dominance as the Purple Moor Grass *Molinia caerulea* moves in, together with a number of more delicate plants. This softer, more diverse vegetation is known as litter because of its use as animal bedding. Unfortunately, it is today uneconomic to mow the fens and the whole process of succession is going on apace and already even the Saw Sedge is on the retreat as the fens are invaded by trees to become carr.

It is therefore little wonder that it did not occur to people to question the natural origin of these open tracts of water. It was primarily the work of two ecologists, Dr. Joyce Lambert of Southampton University and Dr. J. N. Jennings of Leicester, which proved the Broads to be man-made.

The essence of the proof lay in detailed study of the profiles of the peat along carefully levelled transects which ran across the river valleys. If you have ever tried to walk very far through reedswamp, sedge or carr, you will understand the amount of physical effort involved in such a task, not to mention the hours of laboratory work which was required. The effort was, however, well worth it because it showed that the real sides of the Broads were vertical, just like the sides of a shallow quarry. This is of course exactly what the Broads are, flooded peat quarries, or, to use the proper term, cutaways. In the time since they were dug out and re-flooded much new growth has taken place, partly filling the cutaway, obscuring the vertical edges. The proof came by ageing the peat taken from the old floor of the cutaway and that taken from the top of the original edge. There was a great chunk, a chunk of history, missing. The secondary peats and silts which now cover the floor of the cutaways are much younger. The only logical explanation is that it had been removed by man. Delving back into the archives and historical records, from the Domesday Book to the parish records of more modern times, has allowed much of the story to be pieced together and the detailed account of it makes exciting reading. The sheer size of the operations make it a fantastic feat of engineering even by modern standards let alone those of the middle ages. It's one of those peculiar facts that most people know about fantastic achievements of other nations, like the Pyramids and the Great Wall of China, but know virtually

The Broads as they could have looked soon after the last Glacial Period. The photograph is of part of the Mackenzie Delta in North Canada.

Simplified Section across two broads to show some of the evidence proving they were man-made.

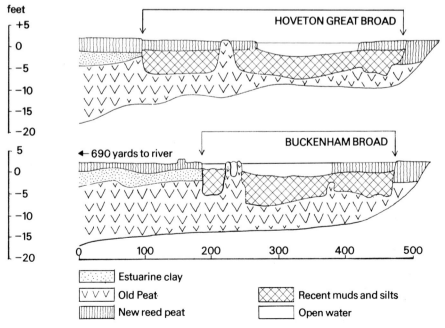

Estuarine clay	
Old Peat	Recent muds and silts
New reed peat	Open water

nothing of what our own forefathers accomplished. We, the original We, the Angles dug that lot. I suppose We also built Hadrian's Wall, at least with a bit of positive prompting from the Romans.

The pattern of use of the Broads has gradually changed as the landscape itself has changed. At the end of the last glaciation it was left as bare lands draining the last of the melt waters to the fast rising North Sea. Its open waters must have been a magnet to birds who came as summer migrants, visitors to the short arctic summer. The weird cry of the Great Northern Diver or Loon must have reverberated around the original lakes. Slowly the green mantle of fenland covered the frost shattered, water worked landscape and the developing peat began to fill the lakes, choking the rivers and impeding water flow through their valleys. In this way more land was flooded and thus in time more fenland created.

Man came to the area, first as a hunter living on the diverse wildlife of the swamps, gradually learning enough about the environment to manipulate small parts of it to grow his crops. It was probably this period which saw the destruction of much of the forests. By this time the bulk of the natural lakes and ponds had disappeared and the only safe method for rapid transport was along the winding rivers. It was along these rivers that the peat from the great turbaries was taken to wherever fuel was required. For, although it must have been in the main a home-based industry, there is little doubt that some of it was used in the manufacture of salt. Once coal mining, linked to barge transport, became the order of the fuel the turbaries, now filled with water, were forgotten and left for new peat to grow.

Once again the natural order held sway and Moorhen, Coot, Bittern, Grebe and all manner of waterfowl went about their business in the thick reedbeds. If I had to choose a plant which is to me the essence of the Broads it would be the Common Reed, *Phragmites australis*. Its specific name is enough to show you just how widespread this plant is, so it cannot be regarded as a good indicator for the Broadland. It is, however, the best signpost for anyone sailing the dykes. The Common Reed is a grass and, like all grasses, its leaf consists of two parts, a long blade which arises from a sheath which encircles the stem. The inside of the sheath of this particular grass is so highly polished that when the wind blows it spins the leaf around so that it trails out on the leeside of the stem. This is not only advantageous to the plant in reducing wind damage, but is a good spot check for the sailor as to exactly what the wind is doing down at the next corner. The extensive beds of Reeds are also the nearest thing nature has ever produced to a farmer's crop, a monoculture which can only thrive by regular addition of fertilizers. In the case of the Reed these are brought in by the rich waters of the river.

The fens thus passed from their main period of industrial development to become, once more, a part of the pastoral scene. Reeds were collected for thatching and the fens were mown for litter and for fodder, often changing the natural pattern of monocultures of Reed and Saw Sedge into polycultures within which many beautiful herbs found niches in which to grow. Times were changing and perhaps the best sign of this change is the dual role of the windpump of Breydon Water, which not only lifted water but ground fish bones to make concrete. More than anything else concrete is the sign of modern man. The windpumps were gradually replaced by diesel fumes which became too much even for the Wherries. No longer was it economic to mow the fens and once more they could have been forgotten, but for the Hullabaloos. This is Arthur Ransome's term for the holiday makers who seek out the new and most lucrative potential of these disused peat quarries – RECREATION. Every year more and more come, and who can blame them, to enjoy this watery wilderness which is not 100 miles from London.

The pressure is on and it is not only the shy wild life that suffers. Already stringent antipollution measures are in operation and there is talk of limiting the fleet. The resource is full to overflowing. One answer has been suggested and that is to dig some new Broads. We've had Plant a Tree Year, how about Dig a Broad Year? Just think what we could do with all those mechanical shovels and with all the peat we took out!

The New Potential – South Walsham Broad, with the dyke leading to the River Bure.

Until this happens we must be thankful that many pieces of our fenland are now nature reserves, the most famous being Wicken Fen, which is looked after for the Nation by the National Trust. The sedge is mown and the lodes and the droves are maintained, the ironical thing being that the Wicken windpump no longer pumps water out of the fen, but lifts water from the dykes which criss-cross the wasted soils up into the fen to keep it going. Wicken Fen is an island of nature standing proud above a sea of ordered farmland. If it wasn't for the regular input of water from the dykes it would be a desert island.

Wicken Fen is without doubt the most unnatural bit of natural Britain, but it is also special in another way, because much of the early work which gave us our understanding of how the fenland ecosystem works was carried out there. Fenlands and Knighthoods must go together, first Sir Cornelius Vermuyden then Sir Arthur Tansley the botanist who worked in the fens, first coined the word ecosystem and wrote the twin volumes "The British Islands and their Vegetation". Then, more recently, Sir Harry Godwin who wrote extensively on the "Natural History of Wicken Fen" and was knighted for his life work, which is still unravelling the History of the British Flora. It would, I feel, be fitting for a modern historian to write an account of the Heraldry of the fens and a good title would be one first coined by, I believe, Professor W. H. Pearsal, a co-worker of the 'two Sirs', "The Fen is greater than the Sward".

Adjacent to Wicken and separated only by Wicken Lode is Adventurers Fen, which commemorates, at least in name, the Magnificent Fourteen who set their hands to the pumps and, there is no getting away from the fact, did a good job draining the flatlands. I can't help wondering what they will be saying about our efforts in three hundred years time.